MAN A MACHINE

and

MAN A PLANT

by

Julien Offray de La Mettrie

Translator's Note: This is a translation of the version of *L'Homme machine* that appeared in La Mettrie's *Oeuvres philosophiques* (Berlin 1751), which Fayard has recently reprinted. In the translation we have retained La Mettrie's sometimes unconventional spellings and capitalizations of proper names; the Notes, however, use the now generally accepted versions.

For assistance with this translation we thank Paul Coppock, Justin Leiber, Michel Rybalka, and most gratefully Alan Gabbey.

Justin Leiber thanks, for their help, David Brown, Paul Coppock, Craig Larson, and Richard Watson.

MAN A MACHINE
and
MAN A PLANT

by

Julien Offray de La Mettrie

Translated by

Richard A. Watson and Maya Rybalka

Introduction and Notes by

Justin Leiber

Hackett Publishing Company, Inc.
Indianapolis/Cambridge

Julien Offray de La Mettrie: 1709–1751

Printed in the United States of America

00 99 98 97 96 2 3 4 5 6 7

Cover design by Listenberger & Associates
Text design by Dan Kirklin

For further information please address

Hackett Publishing Company, Inc.
P.O. Box 44937
Indianapolis, Indiana 46244-0937

Library of Congress Cataloging-in-Publication Data

La Mettrie, Julien Offray de, 1709–1751.
[Homme machine. English]
Man a machine; and, Man a plant/Julien Offray de La Mettrie; translated by Richard A. Watson and Maya Rybalka; new introduction by Justin Leiber.
p. cm.
Includes bibliographical references and index.
ISBN 0-87220-195-3. ISBN 0-87220-194-5 (pbk.)
1. Materialism—Early works to 1800. 2. Physiology—Early works to 1800. 3. Mind and body—Early works to 1800. 4. Mechanism (Philosophy)—Early works to 1800. I. La Mettrie, Julien Offray de, 1709–1751. Homme plante. English. II. Title.
B2063.H513 1994
128—dc20 94-29259
CIP

The paper used in this publication meets the minimum requirements of American National Standard for Information Sciences—Permanence of Paper for Printed Library Materials, ANSI Z39.48—1984.

∞

INTRODUCTION

L'Homme machine (*Man a Machine*) was published in 1748 anonymously, with good reason, considering its brazen thesis. Its author, Julien de La Mettrie, argues that animals are machines and that humans are animals and so are machines as well. Claiming that this conclusion derives from Descartes, La Mettrie also attacks a certain "M. Charp" who recently had derided Descartes's demonstration that animals are machines. Yet "M. Charp" is none other than La Mettrie himself. How to explain this byzantine and operatic circumstance?

Using his dictum "I think; therefore I am," René Descartes (1596–1650) provides a compelling metaphysical rationalization for the view that human souls are different from matter, that we survive the death of our body, and that the notion that we are simply complicated biological mechanisms is absurd. I call Descartes's argument a *rationalization* because he realized that advances in anatomy, biology, and neurophysiology might well be thought to have begun to form a firm scientific basis for materialism. This echoes Sigmund Freud's claim that paranoia is a *caricature* of Cartesian philosophy: the paranoid's egotistical constructions bewitch only himself, while Descartes's dualism captivated philosophy well into this century.

Descartes stood in need of such a rationalization in that he himself did much of the anatomical and neurological work that led to La Mettrie's materialism. Descartes, notoriously, showed in detail that animals are complicated machines and that human bodies can be studied as machines as well. After the persecution of Galileo, however, Descartes prudently suppressed his mechanistic writings on the world and man. A hundred years later, on the basis of many further advances in physiology, Julien Offray de La Mettrie (1709–1751) argued that man, like other animals an evolutionary product of nature, is a machine, controlled by neurological mechanisms in the brain.

Early in his teens, La Mettrie turned away from a talent for poetry and oratory to Jansenism, a puritanical, mystical, fatalistic, and beleaguered movement in French Catholicism. According to Frederick the Great, he wrote a book, now lost, which became popular with Jansenists. In his middle teens, La Mettrie attended the College d'Harcourt, where the previously banned works of Descartes had just been added to its curriculum. In his late teens, La Mettrie began five years at the Faculté de médecine of Paris, took his doctor's degree at the University of Rheims, and went on to postdoctoral study at Leyden. He then took up a medical practice in his native city of St. Malo and moved to Paris in 1742.

In 1745, La Mettrie published *Histoire naturelle de l'âme* (*The Natural History of the Soul*), in which he defends a guarded materialism. He appropriates the well-established Aristotelian and Scholastic doctrine of "substantial forms" to argue that organic matter has not only the "passive" and "mechanical" properties that Descartes attributes to it, but also "active" and "formal" properties that include feeling and thought. At the same time, he emphasizes observation and experiment as the only secure way to truth, and, on pragmatic grounds, he strongly recommends mechanical explanations. Sounding a theme to which he returns throughout his career, La Mettrie stresses the similarities among plants, animals, and human beings. And since, in the *Histoire naturelle de l'âme,* he makes the politic assumption that man is more than a machine, plants and animals must be more than machines as well. La Mettrie prudently adds to his title page: "translated from the English of M. Charp, by the late M. H*** of the Academie des Sciences." Nevertheless, the publication soon cost him his post as medical officer of the Gardes Français, with whom he had served in the War of the Austrian Succession at the bloody battles of Dettingen (June 27, 1743) and Fontenoy (May 11, 1745), and the siege of Freiburg (Fall, 1744). Frederick the Great says that at Freiberg, in the aftermath of a raging fever, La Mettrie

> could clearly see that thought is but a consequence of the organization of the machine, and that the disturbance of the springs has considerable influence on that part of us which the metaphysicians call soul . . . he tried to explain by the aid of anatomy the thin texture of understanding, and he found only mechanism where others had supposed an essence superior to matter. (Bussey, p. 6)

Temporarily undaunted by the dismissal from his regiment, La Mettrie managed to win promotion to medical director of the military hospitals of the campaign. However, on July 9, 1746, the Parliament of Paris condemned *The Natural History of the Soul* to be burned by the public hangman. Earlier that year, La Mettrie had anonymously published an attack on the greed and incompetence of French physicians, *Politique du médecin de Machiavel* (*Politics of Machiavelli's Doctor*). With both clerics and doctors out to destroy him, La Mettrie fled on the advice of the Duke of Duras and the Viscount of Chaila (cf. Frederick's *Éloge*).

In the early fall of 1746, thirty-six year old Julien Offray de La Mettrie fled to Holland, where he had studied at the University of Leyden, the preeminent medical center of Europe, under its most noted professor, Hermann Boerhaave. From 1735 to 1741, La Mettrie had painstakingly translated Boerhaave's multivolumed medical texts into French, adding his own extensive commentaries, as part of his effort to reform and demystify French medicine. To the same end, La Mettrie also published *Observations de médecine pratique* (1743) and studies on vertigo and venereal disease.

Would the man who has been variously credited as the first truly modern materialist, the first modern defender of animal rights, the first modern sexologist and criminologist, now draw in his horns? No. To quote from Aram Vartanian's critical edition of *L'Homme machine*, p. 6,

> La Mettrie was not a man who could long cower under persecution, or let a challenge go unanswered. With a boldness of spirit which was surely foolhardy under the circumstances, and which was rarely to find its equal among his fellow philosophes, he struck back zestfully against both the charlatans and the bigots who had driven him from his native land. During 1747 La Mettrie composed against the former the ironic comedy, *La Faculté vengée* [The Doctors' Revenge], and against the latter, *L'Homme machine*.

The book you hold is thus the passionate outpouring of a reformed puritan, of a man who has had enough of masks and caution, of all the rationalizations designed to conciliate science and medicine with the forces of received opinion by obscuring science and disarming effective medical practice. Instead of a deism designed to convert religious fervor into orderly citizenship, La Mettrie offers open atheism. Instead of incorrigible first person inner experience, La Mettrie *begins* with man the machine, whose cognitive character, like that of animals, is "so little incompatible with organized matter it seems to be one of its properties on a par with electricity, the faculty of motion, penetrability, extension, etc." Rather than the "blank tablet" mind, which suggests both the perfectibility of human beings and their complete malleability, La Mettrie finds, both in individuals and in species, a range of inherited and inborn anatomical and neurological features, compulsions and limitations. On these bases, disordered and criminal individuals deserve treatment and cure more than punishment. Further, we should seek to satisfy our native drives for pleasure, rather than vainly trying to eradicate them. Hence, too, the remorse that sensitive humans feel after sensual gratification or questionable behavior is often more pathological than salutary.

La Mettrie probably completed *L'Homme machine* in August, 1747. By early December, copies of its first printing by the Leyden publisher Elie Luzac were circulating. On December 18, Elie Luzac was called before the Consistory of the Church of Leyden and ordered to deliver all copies of *L'Homme machine* for burning, to reveal the identity of the anonymous author, and to promise never again to commit such an offense. Although he apparently promised to comply with the first and the last of these demands, Luzac claimed, possibly truly, that he did not know who wrote the book. And while he did deliver some of the error-ridden first printing for burning, he also produced a corrected second and third printing in 1748, to meet the rapidly growing demand for the book. Then he prudently left the country. In the second printing of *L'Homme machine,* Elie Luzac added at the end of his "Warning from the Printer" a paragraph explicitly stating that he does not know who wrote the book he is publishing.

Before the first printing of *L'Homme machine,* La Mettrie had corresponded with Maupertuis, whom Frederick the Great had made head of the Berlin Academy of the Sciences in 1746. Maupertuis, a mathematician and champion of Newtonian physics, grew up, like La Mettrie, in the isolated northwestern coastal town of St. Malo. La Mettrie dedicated *The Natural History of the Soul* to Maupertuis and probably had the six copies of *L'Homme machine* forwarded to D'Argens so Frederick and his group of resident intellectuals might sample it. In any case, La Mettrie wrote to accept Frederick's protection on January 7, 1748. Rumors that he was the author of *L'Homme machine* were circulating in Holland by the end of the month, and La Mettrie had to leave immediately, arriving in Berlin on February 7, 1748.

La Mettrie got on unusually well with Frederick, who gave him a pension, made him his official physician and a member of the Academy of Science, and allowed him an easy and most unusual personal familiarity that undoubtedly made some of Frederick's circle jealous, including Voltaire and D'Argens, who maligned La Mettrie after his premature death in 1751. While he spent enough time at Frederick's palace of Sans Souci to underwrite the subsequent caricature of him as a mad, chuckling, bright-eyed propounder of racy and irreligious paradoxes, La Mettrie continued to write, publishing treatises on dysentery and asthma, and writing *L'Homme plante, Système d'Epicure, Abrégé des systèmes*. These, together with *L'Homme machine* and related works including two on sexual fulfillment, were published as his *Oeuvres philosophiques* (Berlin 1751; followed by at least ten Berlin and Amsterdam reprintings over the next fifteen years).

La Mettrie also continued his medical practice. In October, 1751, he brought the Irish-born French Ambassador to Prussia, Tirconnel, through some illness. Impulsively, the Ambassador's wife invited La Mettrie to dine. Supposedly after eating a pastry encrusted pâté, La Mettrie collapsed into a high fever and delirium, dying some twenty days later on November 11. Although it had no factual foundation, the gloating caricature soon circulated of the libertine sensualist dying in gluttonous ecstasy. Perhaps inevitably, contrary to all contemporary accounts, to that story was soon added a recital of his miraculous deathbed conversion. Of this last story, Vartanian remarks, p. 12,

> But these must surely be dismissed as pious fabrications, for Frederick II made a point of finding out just how the philosophe had fared *in extremis*, and only on being assured that he had met with an honorable end did His Majesty deign to compose personally the *Éloge de La Mettrie* and have it read before the Berlin Academy.

In his detailed account of La Mettrie, now virtually the only primary source aside from La Mettrie's publications, Frederick concludes that, "All those who are not imposed upon by the pious insults of the theologians mourn in La Mettrie a good man and a wise physician" [Bussey, p. 9]. Alas, Frederick mourned alone.

In his novel *Catch-22*, Joseph Heller introduced the transitive use of "disappear" as in "They disappeared Dunbar." It is hard to think of a more successful job of disappearing than that done to La Mettrie, who in the 1740s forged the biologically oriented materialism, evolutionism, and ethical naturalism hesitatingly, often secretly, expressed by the *philosophes* of the 1770s—Diderot in particular—only to have his work and person absurdly and wantonly caricatured by both the *antiphilosophes* and *philosophes* of the 1750s and '60s. With more than a dozen printings his work was widely available but under-the-counter, unmentionable in polite, scientific, and scholarly society. But knowledge of it faded as fashion changed, leaving only the picture of the libertine atheist and his fateful pâté. After the many printings of *Man a Machine* in English in 1749–50, there were no more until the 1912 translation of Bussey, who left out some two hundred lines in which La Mettrie mentions genitalia, human reproduction, and fetal development. *L'Homme machine*, after Luzac's three printings of 1748, did not reappear as a single volume in French until J. Assézat's scholarly edition published in 1865. *Oeuvres philosophiques* was finally republished by Fayard in 1987, some two hundred years after the last of the many printings of the 1750s and '60s. Thus, until the last few decades, La Mettrie was disappeared from histories of the Enlightenment, except for some humorous lines about his chatter with Frederick and his untimely death. Lytton Strachey, who really should have known better, could not resist writing that

> [La Mettrie] made his escape in a different manner—by dying after supper one evening of a surfeit of pheasant pie. 'Jésus! Marie!' he gasped, as he felt the pains of death upon him. 'Ah!' said a priest who had been sent for, 'vous voilà enfin retourné à ces noms consolateurs' [''Ah, thus you finally return to these consoling names'']. La Mettrie, with an oath, expired: and Frederick, on hearing of this unorthodox conclusion, remarked, 'J'en suis bien aise, pour le repos de son âme' [''I am very glad of it, for the repose of his soul'']. (1948, p. 95–96)

With an irony that would likely have delighted La Mettrie, Friedrich Lange, the first scholar forthrightly to assign La Mettrie his proper place as the first modern materialist and source of the main ideas of the *philosophes*, did so in his *History of Materialism and Critique of Its Present Significance* (1866), a Kantian work in which Lange displays materialism as a naive scientistic dogma, a dubious vogue of French origins, now safely refuted and in decline. Professor Lange protests that La Mettrie is ''one of the most abused, but one of the least read, authors in the history of literature." Nonetheless, the good Professor found La Mettrie's assertion (or mention, perhaps) of sexual pleasure abhorrent and (to note what seems to be his most fundamental criticism of him) *frivolous*:

> In common with most of these French philosophers, he found only people who loved the debaucheries of sensuality as much as he did, and who only took care not to write books about it. La Mettrie may be frivolous, and this is a serious charge, but he neither sent his children to the Foundling like Rousseau, nor betrayed two girls, like Swift; he was not convicted of corruption, like Bacon, nor does the suspicion of forgery rest upon his name as upon Voltaire's. (Section 4, p. 79)

We can appreciate La Mettrie today in part because we share his views about the importance of sexual fulfillment and the need for medical treatment for mental ills, but even more because we must come to grips with the evident sense in which we are animals. Rightly or wrongly, we are beginning to think of ourselves as biological thinking machines. We are also trying to make artificial thinking machines. Perhaps because of this, we are coming to grips with our affinities with, and responsibilities toward, our fellow animal and plant machines as well. Today, Mr. Machine, as La Mettrie manically dubbed himself, finally has his audience.

II

More specifically, what are La Mettrie's claims and what was new about his materialism?

Modern anatomical and neurological studies, even before La Mettrie's day, far exceeded classical learning. A critical step in this advance, as Leonardo da Vinci, Descartes, and others saw it, was the discovery of mechanical explanations for bodily functions. The central example for the time is Harvey's explanation of the heart and circulatory system as pump and tubing, which required postulation of capillaries whose existence was confirmed by microscopy four years after Harvey's death in 1657. Indeed, the advance from classical to modern technology was spectacular. Clocks and clockwork had long fascinated modern imagination, while telescopes and microscopes revealed macrocosm and microcosm. La Mettrie was impressed by Vaucanson's ingenious mechanical duck and mechanical flute player, and even more by Huyghens' planetarium, a mechanical model of the movements of a solar system presented by modern physicists as a smoothly running machine. It had become possible to take seriously the thought that man is an automated machine that winds its own springs.

La Mettrie refers to the number and variety of ways in which the "soul" is affected by disease, sleep, drugs, food, age, sex, temperature, and climate. Further, and more importantly, recent neurological workers, including La Mettrie, had begun to search out systematically how perception, cognition, and behavior are subserved by different parts of the brain and are differentially affected by *localized* brain damage or genetically inherited abnormality. While La Mettrie is the first to assert explictly and systematically that the whole man is a machine, he articulates a scientific paradigm already implicit in much of the work he cites. His is an experimentally and pragmatically sanctioned materialism.

Two recent discoveries particularly animated La Mettrie's materialism: Albrecht Haller's work on muscular irritability and, most crucially, Abraham Trembley's investigation of the freshwater polyp. Before Haller it was supposed that nerves are hollow and convey "animal spirits" that animate muscles. Haller shows that direct stimulus to the muscle produces local animation and that the same stimulus to a nerve leading to a muscle causes a much more powerful effect. Far from being "passive matter," muscles have an animation of their own; the nerves transfer a signal to this mechanism. Thought, too, La Mettrie asserts, is "a property of matter" on a par with "electricity, the faculty of motion, etc."

When La Mettrie imagines a craftsman making a "talking man," he dubs him "a new Prometheus," which Mary Shelley echoes seventy years later in her *Frankenstein, or The Modern Prometheus*. Shelley finds the prospect ominous, but La Mettrie views this prospect with as much enthusiasm as Alan Turing in 1950. Materialism is often presented soberly as providing a gray, austerely mechanical world, but La Mettrie eroticizes nature as a world of color and joy, a blooming and budding kaleidoscopic biosphere.

In 1744, Abraham Trembley published an account of his experimental investigation of the freshwater polyp. Leeuwenhoeck classified the small, tubular, gelatinous creature, which normally reproduces through shoots, as a plant. Trembley noticed that the armlike tentacles capture food and convey it to the mouthlike opening that leads to a stomach. This suggests that the polyp is also an animal (its present classification). Most significantly, one can section a polyp into many scores of pieces and each carries on as a separate organism, growing, moving, eating, sprouting, etc. This discovery fueled La Mettrie's conversion to the forthright mechanistic materialism of *L'Homme machine* and *L'Homme plante*, for it suggests continuity between plants and animals. Even more significantly, if by splitting a polyp into scores of bits you can create as many living (animated, ensouled) organisms as you wish, then life is a property of matter, not a mysterious second substance or soul. Trembley's polyp had a significance in his time comparable to commissurotomy in our own. (In the 1960s, surgeons successfully treated very severe epilepsy by severing the corpus callosum that connects the two cerebral hemispheres. Michael Gazzaniga and others investigated an unexpected side effect of this commissurotomy: under highly contrived experimental conditions, some patients exhibit two separate personalities and cognitive centers housed in the respective hemispheres. This strongly suggests that mind is a property of the brain, not of some independent substance that happens to be somehow correlated, or running in parallel, with the brain.) The great impact of Trembley's polyp is strikingly illustrated by Diderot's use of it, over two decades later, as the centerpiece of his confident materialism in *Le Rêve D'Alembert.*

La Mettrie stands, in another important respect, as a link between classical materialism and the materialism that has become dominant in recent philosophy. La Mettrie simply refuses to take Cartesian methodological doubt seriously. When Bertrand Russell introduced the English translation of Professor Lange's *History of Materialism* (1925), Russell confidently asserted that spiritualism and materialism were both unsupported dogmas. Comfortably following the then so familiar route, Russell reasoned as follows: I cannot be wholly confident in my knowledge of either supernatural entities, other minds, or material objects, although I am of course wholly confident that I know the contents and features of the subjective world of my "immediate experience." Hence mental experience definitely exists, and perhaps my body exists also, but the mental and material are necessarily distinguishable and, while there may be various correlations between them, the one cannot be the other, except in the sense in which physical objects might be "logical constructions" out of "sense data," etc.

While La Mettrie pays lip service to classical skepticism, "to avoid any dispute with the Pyrrhonians," he simply refuses to take up the specific skepticism about our knowledge of the material world that Descartes's *Meditations* bequeathed to the subsequent tradition that led, through Locke, Berkeley, Leibniz, and Kant, down to Russell.

> Not that I think for a moment that our senses always deceive us as Father Malebranche has claimed, or that our eyes are by nature a little drunk and do not see objects as they are in themselves. (p. 84)

Indeed, La Mettrie might be taken to announce his disdain for this tradition on the first page of *Man a Machine.*

> Strictly speaking, to ask if matter sheerly in itself can think is to ask if matter can keep time. We see in advance that we will avoid this reef, on which Mr. Locke had the misfortune to run aground. (p. 63)

Following a highly dubious tradition, La Mettrie had applauded Locke in *Histoire naturelle de l'âme* as a covert and cautious materialist, one who argues that God certainly *could* have made thought a property of matter. As Aran Vartanian explains La Mettrie's new charge against Locke,

> If in 1748 La Mettrie's mistaken notion of what Locke had meant to say was not changed, he at least criticized it as a badly conceived version of materialism. While, on the one hand, Locke was now supposed to have said that thought is a general *metaphysical* property of matter, and, owing to its theological origin, an unintelligible property besides; *L'Homme machine*, on the other hand, regarded thought as a specifically *mechanical* property of matter, hence as the object of scientific explanation. (1960, p. 205; but see also Yolton [1991] for a fuller account.)

Indeed, as Vartanian goes on to point out, Locke in fact argues, just as the Cartesians, that it is a simple truth of reason that matter cannot think. To the contrary, as La Mettrie briskly sets the experimentalist scientific and neurological agenda, the real problem is to see how nature does the job, how matter is organized into mind.

> Man is a machine so complicated that it is impossible at first to form a clear idea of it, and consequently to define it. This is why all the *a priori* investigations of the greatest philosophers, their attempts to take

> flight with the wings of the mind, have been in vain. Only *a posteriori*, by unravelling the soul as one pulls out the guts of the body, can one, I do not say prove what the nature of man is, but rather attain the highest degree of probability possible on the subject. (p. 67)

Some people will do anything—as La Mettrie gently mocks—to avoid the *shame* of having a soul of mud, a mind characterized by scientific naturalism. Dramatizing the opposite view, La Mettrie embraces nature and the continuity between humans, nonhuman animals, plants, and man-made devices. He glorifies the wonders of organized matter, of machines.

> To be a machine, to feel, think, know how to tell good from evil like blue from yellow, in a word, to be born with intelligence and a sure instinct for morality, and yet to be only an animal, are things no more contradictory than to be an ape or a parrot and to know how to find sexual pleasure. (p. 112)

La Mettrie emphasizes the close relationship between the complexity of an animal's behavior and the size of its brain. The human animal has the largest brain (compared to body size) and the longest period of infancy and maturation, depends the most on learning and development and the least on instinct. La Mettrie notes that the chimpanzee, closest to human in ratio of brain to body size, is also the most similar in cognitive attainments (while La Mettrie writes of the "orangutan," it seems most probable that he means the chimpanzee). He notes that chimpanzees can gesture and mimic, and he speculates that it might well be possible to teach them to speak a human language. And the speculation is hardly idle, for, ever the experimentalist, La Mettrie makes some very practical and prescient suggestions as to how the experiment should be run, such as training apes through the use of gestural techniques already employed with human deaf mutes, preference for young apes as more educable subjects, etc.

Indeed, this is a central point for La Mettrie because, like Descartes, he believes that language is the major feature that separates socialized humans from nonhuman animals. Human minds differ from animal minds because human minds are stuffed with words and figures in addition to all that they have in common with animal minds. Language allows us to "polish" a mind that would otherwise be less able than that of many other animals. As well as the issue of teaching apes language, this also raises the issue of how language-deprived humans develop (La Mettrie wrote half a century before the wild boy of Aveyron but he does mention a wild girl). La Mettrie extolls the work of Johann Amman, who devoted himself to teaching deaf mutes to speak by drawing their attention to the motion of his lips, tongue, and larynx, and getting them to imitate his activity. Although La Mettrie employs the evocative phrase "in their eyes he discovered ears," the discovery that full-fledged sign language could have something like the conceptual power of spoken language came more than half a century later. Ironically, recent studies of spoken and signed language have made it clear that they share many powerful, nonarbitrary features that are rooted in human neurophysiology. Attempts to teach apes sign language have revealed much more of a discontinuity than La Mettrie expected.

The *philosophes* distinguished themselves from other philosophers in that they reject epistemological doubt and happily merge their work with science and technology as a collective enterprise for the improvement of human lives. If Diderot is the most representative and historically commanding *philosophe*, La Mettrie is the first.

While Diderot (1711–84) was born only three years after La Mettrie, Diderot lived and wrote for several decades after La Mettrie's early death. Many of Diderot's most audacious and materialist writings, sometimes shared with a correspondence circle, were published only in the 1830s, many years after his death. Ironically, when he wrote *Le Rêve D'Alembert* in 1769, many would still have been familiar with La Mettrie's infamous use of Trembley's polyp, and perhaps some still in 1782 when Diderot distributed *Le Rêve D'Alembert* in correspondence. But by the time it was published in 1830, few could have made the connection. Nonetheless, there are respects in which La Mettrie is more modern and more materialist than Diderot.

La Mettrie is the more pessimistic about the possibility that education might greatly change human character or wholly correct individual biological abnormalities. La Mettrie disdained "innate ideas" insofar as they are meant to constitute the immaterial substance of the soul. But he obviously believed that a good portion of our cognition is structured by our inherited neurophysiology.

Diderot directly clashes with La Mettrie about the health and moral efficacy of remorse. In *L'Homme machine*, La Mettrie presupposes the then nearly universal view that remorse is essential to morality and human society, and he is at pains to argue that nonhuman animals feel remorse as well, indeed that they exhibit remorse much as humans do and that the explanation for and identification of this emotion in them is also much the same as in humans. In a subsequent work, *Discours sur le bonheur* (*Discourse on Happiness*), La Mettrie emphasizes that remorse is not very effective because it occurs *after* undesirable behavior. Further, if society were to foster guilt less, perhaps some scoundrels would sleep better, but many more wise and virtuous persons would no longer be tormented by an overly puritanical education. Indeed, La Mettrie criticizes the Stoics, then much admired, and Seneca in particular, for disdaining pleasure and warmth of feeling. It is for this view particularly that Diderot lambastes La Mettrie in his *Essai sur les règnes de Claude et Néron*, published thirty years after La Mettrie's death.

Ironically, the once disdained and defamed La Mettrie has been acclaimed, and claimed, by a variety of historians and for a variety of causes over the last several decades. In her scholarly *From Beast-Machine to Man-Machine: Animal Soul in French Letters from Descartes to La Mettrie* (1940), Rosenfield sees *L'Homme machine* as the decisive climax of a major chapter in human thought, one which, rather than degrading man, justly elevates the status of animals and a utilitarian social philosophy as well. In a similar vein but with more detailed attention to the humane treatment of nonhuman animals, in her *Man and Beast in French Thought of the Eighteenth Century* (1936), Hastings sees *L'Homme machine* as the decisive culmination of Descartes's beast-machine hypothesis and demonstrations, and La Mettrie as

> The first great French materialist of the eighteenth century. . . . No longer does he appear as the echo of great thinkers. On the contrary, he is seen to express ideas for which Buffon, Rousseau, Helvetius, and d'Holbach are specifically famous. (p. 95)

In her *La Mettrie: Medicine, Philosophy, and Enlightenment* (1992), Wellman provides a full and well-researched account of La Mettrie's whole career as physician-*philosophe*, of his Boerhaave translations and commentaries, and his well-warranted war with the medical establishment. Wellman, possibly overdoing the continuity between La Mettrie's *Natural History of the Soul* and *Man a Machine*, argues for disregarding La Mettrie's embrace of Descartes's mechanistic views and rejection of Locke in *Man a Machine*. Let the reader judge.

In 1960, Vartanian published the masterful critical edition, *La Mettrie's "L'Homme machine": A Study in the History of an Idea.* In his *Descartes and Diderot: A Study of Scientific Naturalism in the Enlightenment* (1953) and in several of his essays, Vartanian amply enhances Rosenfield's and Hastings's view that *L'Homme machine* is the decisive culmination of Descartes's beast-machine work. More generally, he concludes that the materialism of the *philosophes* derives from Descartes's mechanistic views and his rejection of final causes, and not from Locke and Newton. Unfortunately, as Noam Chomsky has pointed out, the *philosophes* failed to see that when they discarded the methodological doubt and substance dualism of *Meditations*, they might well have retained Descartes's well-supported nativist claims about language and cognition.

Audaciously and impishly, La Mettrie writes that Descartes's dualism is a "sleight of hand" that Descartes designed to shield himself from the full fury of clerical attack on his thinly veiled materialism. Perhaps what led La Mettrie to this wildly paradoxical suggestion is that, in the decades following his death, Descartes's critics level by far their most vehement attacks on his claim that animals are machines, and these assaults seem motivated not by love of animals but by a fear that such a line of thought would eventually call into question the status of humans as well. What is true is that, immediately upon hearing of the persecution of Galileo, Descartes did suppress *Le Monde*, in which he adopts the heliocentric view of the solar system. In this work he treats at length, if only hypothetically, of human bodies as machines. And this is enough for Lindeboom in his *Descartes and Medicine* (1979), e.g., to treat Descartes as the originator of the machine-model to the study of human anatomy, and thus as the father of scientific naturalism.

Descartes's once triumphant metaphysical dualism now seems doubtful and is certainly unpopular in the Anglo-American world today. But there are two Descarteses: the solipsist Descartes of *Meditations* and the mechanistic experimentalist of *Le Monde* and many other writings. La Mettrie reconstructed, extended, and passed on the mechanistic Descartes, which is to say he gave full expression to the larger and more disconcerting implications of scientific naturalism. The reader can decide which Cartesianism—La Mettrie's materalism or Russell's dualism—has been the more important, helpful, legitimate, or true. What is undeniable is the Rabelaisian mirth, the cheery collegiality, the infectious enthusiasm, and finally the triumphant defiance, with which La Mettrie puts forward his views, views that are now commonplaces of today's materialism and naturalism.

Justin Leiber
University of Houston

Short Bibliography

Bergmann, Ernst (1913). *Die Satiren des Herrn Maschine, ein Beitrag zur Philosophie und Kulturgeschichte des 18. Jhr.* Leipzig: E. Wiegandt.

Bussey, G. C. (1912). *Man a Machine.* Chicago: Open Court. (Contains French and English versions, and a translation of Frederick's *Éloge.*)

Chomsky, Noam (1966). *Cartesian Linguistics: A Chapter in the History of Rationalist Thought.* New York: Harper & Row.

Dennett, D. (1991). *Consciousness Explained.* Boston: Little, Brown.

Descartes, René (1979/1641). *Meditations.* Trans. Haldane, E. D.; Ross, G. R. T., *The Philosophical Works of Descartes.* Cambridge: The University Press.

Frederick the Great (1753). *Éloges de trois philosophes.* London.

Gazzaniga, Michael (1988). *Mind Matters: How the Mind and Brain Interact to Create Our Conscious Lives.* Boston: Houghton Mifflin.

Hastings, Helen (1936). *Man and Beast in French Thought of the Eighteenth Century.* Baltimore: Johns Hopkins Press.

King, Lester (1978). *The Philosophy of Medicine: The Early Eighteenth Century.* Cambridge, Mass.: Harvard University Press.

La Mettrie, Julien Offray de (1751/1987). *Oeuvres philosophiques.* Londres [Berlin]. Reissued in Paris: Fayard.

Lange, Friedrich (1865/1950). *History of Materialism.* New York: Humanities Press.

Lemée, Pierre (1954). *Julien Offray de La Mettrie, médecin, philosophe, polemiste; sa vie, son oeuvre.* Mortain: Editions Mortainais.

Lindeboom, G. A. (1979). *Descartes and Medicine.* Amsterdam: Editions Rodopi.

Locke, John (1690/1975). *An Essay Concerning Human Understanding.* P. H. Nidditch, ed. Oxford: The Clarendon Press.

Luzac, Elie (1748). *L'homme plus que machine* (Man more than a machine). Leyden.

Needham, Joseph (1928). *Man a Machine, in Answer to a Romantical and Unscientific Treatise Written by Sig. Eugenio Rignan & Entitled "Man Not a Machine."* New York: Norton.

Rosenfield, Leonora (1940/1968). *From Beast-Machine to Man-Machine*. New York: Octagon Books.

Rougier, Francis (1936). *Offray de La Mettrie L'Homme-Plante*. New York: Columbia University Press.

Strachey, Lytton (1948). *Biographical Essays*. London: Chatto and Windus.

Turing, A. (1950). "Computing Machinery and Intelligence." *Mind*, Vol. LIX, No. 236.

Vartanian, Aram (1949). "Elie Luzac's Refutation of La Mettrie." *Modern Language Notes, LXIV*, 159–61.

_____ (1950). "Trembley's Polyp, La Mettrie and Eighteenth Century French Materialism." *Journal of the History of Ideas, XI*, 3, 259–86.

_____ (1952). *Diderot and Descartes, A Study of Scientific Naturalism in the Enlightenment*. Princeton University Press.

_____ (1960). *La Mettrie's "L'Homme machine": A Study in the Origins of an Idea*. Princeton University Press.

_____ (1977). "La Mettrie, Diderot, and Sexology in the Enlightenment." In *Essays in the Age of Enlightenment in Honor of Ira O. Wade*, Jean Macray (ed.), 347-67. Geneva: Droz.

Verbeek, Theo (1988). *"Traite de l'âme" de La Mettrie*. Edited with commentary. Utrecht: OMI-Grafisch Bedrijf.

Wellman, Kathleen (1992). *La Mettrie, Medicine, Philosophy, and Enlightenment*. Durham: Duke University Press.

Yolton, John (1991). *Locke and French Materialism*. Oxford: The Clarendon Press.

First Memoir to Serve as the
55 Natural History of Man

MAN A MACHINE

Preface by the Printer[1]

You will perhaps be surprised to see that I dare attach my name to a book as audacious as this one. I certainly would not have done so if I did not believe that religion is safe from every attempt to overturn it, or had I been able to convince myself that some other printer would not have done with great pleasure what I refused to do on principle of conscience. I know prudence advises that we should never provide opportunities for the seduction of weak minds. But I saw on first reading that there is nothing here to fear even if they were seduced. And anyway, why should we be so vigilant about suppressing arguments contrary to the ideas of divinity and religion? Might this not make people think we are *deceiving* them? And once people begin to doubt, goodbye conviction and in consequence religion! What means or hope could we ever have of confounding the irreligious if we seem to fear them? How could we bring them back to religion if we forbid them the use of their reason and, more or less at random, merely criticize their morals? We had better first ask whether their morals merit the same censure as their way of thinking.

Such caution cedes the case to the unbelievers. They mock a religion that we ignorantly think cannot be conciliated with philoso-

1. The Warning was written by Elie Luzac (1723–1796), a Leyden publisher with a French Protestant background, who presumably published the book for the reasons he states, for he later wrote a refutation of *L'Homme machine*, titled *L'Homme plus que machine* (Man Is More Than a Machine).

phy. They cry victory in their strongholds because our cowardice makes them think themselves invincible. If religion is not victorious, 56
it is the fault of the bad authors who defend it. Let good authors take up the pen, and, well armed, theology will valiantly carry the day against its feeble rivals. Atheists are like those giants who try to climb to heaven: Their fate will always be the same.

I put these remarks at the beginning of this small brochure to forestall anxiety. It would be improper for me to refute what I print, or even to express my opinions about the reasoning in this book. But connoisseurs can easily see that its difficulties are merely those that arise whenever anyone tries to explain the union of body and soul. If the author's conclusions are dangerous, remember that their ground is only a hypothesis. Is anything more required to destroy them? But if you will permit me to present as a supposition something I do not believe, that even if these consequences were difficult to overturn, one would have only a finer occasion to shine. *To vanquish without peril is to triumph without glory.*

57 # To Monsieur Haller, Professor of Medicine, at Göttingen[2]

This is not a dedication. You are far above any eulogy I could give you, and nothing is so dull and useless as the formal discourse of the Academies. Nor is this an exposition of a new method for refurbishing a worn out and hackneyed subject, so my discourse has at least that in its favor. As for the rest, you can judge whether your disciple and friend has done his job well. I want to speak of the pleasure I have had in composing this work. And it is myself, not my book, who speaks to you, to enlighten myself on the nature of this sublime pleasure of study. Such being the subject of this discourse, I would not be the first writer who, having nothing to say, took a text where none had gone before to compensate for the sterility of his

2. The dedication to Albrecht von Haller (1708–1777) undoubtedly sprang from many motives aside from La Mettrie's evident agreement with and respect for Haller's important neurological work, and particularly his demonstrations of muscular irritability. Both were students of Boerhaave at Leyden, although there is no evidence that they were acquainted. La Mettrie translated Haller's annotated edition of Boerhaave's *Institutiones re medicae* into French, weaving Haller's Latin notes into a larger commentary of his own. Although La Mettrie acknowledged Haller's "excellent notes" in his introduction, Haller's name did not appear on the title page as one of the authors. In a review of the book, Haller, with some justification, accused La Mettrie of plagiarism. He renewed this accusation, now quite unfairly, in a subsequent review of La Mettrie's *Histoire naturelle de l'âme* in 1747. The dedication to Haller is La Mettrie's ambiguous response to the second review. Though the dedication of his "friend and disciple" is an exercise in mockingly exaggerated praise with erotic innuendoes that parody a youthful and well-known poem of Haller's, and compares him to Fracastor, who had written in verse about syphilis, the serious-minded Haller did not recognize the sarcasm or the identity of the author in his review. Immediately following publication of *L'Homme machine*, Haller solemnly expressed extreme abhorrence for the views propounded in the book. When it became clear that La Mettrie had written *L'Homme machine*, Haller issued several public denials of any connection with La Mettrie.

imagination. Tell me, then, twofold son of Apollo, illustrious Swiss gentleman, modern Fracastor,[3] you who can instantly know nature, take its measure, what is more, experience it, and even more, express it: Learned physician, even greater poet, tell me by what enchantments study can change hours into moments. What is the nature of these pleasures of the mind that are so different from ordinary pleasures . . . But the reading of your charming poetry has penetrated me too deeply for me not to say what it has inspired. Man, from this point of view, is not foreign to my subject.

However agreeable, cherished, and eulogized by the apparently grateful pen of a young French physician, sensual pleasure has *58*
only one climax, which is the tomb. If complete satisfaction of sensual pleasure does not kill it irretrievably, at least a certain period of time is required to rouse it again. How different are the resourceful pleasures of the mind! The closer one approaches truth, the more charming it becomes. Not only does its enjoyment increase desire, but also one feels pleasure as soon as one seeks it. This pleasure comes in a rush faster than lightning strikes; yet it lasts for a long time. Should one be astonished that the pleasure of the mind is as superior to sensual pleasure as the mind is to the body? Is not the mind the first of the senses, that meeting place of all sensations, on which they converge like rays returning to the center that produces them? Look no farther, then, for those invincible charms that suddenly transport a heart enflamed by the love of truth into a more beautiful world where it enjoys pleasures worthy of the gods. Of all the attractions of nature, the most powerful, at least for me as for you, dear Haller, is philosophy. What finer glory than to be conducted to philosophy's temple by reason and wisdom! No conquest gives more exquisite pleasure than the submission of oneself to them.

Pass in review all these pleasures unknown to common souls. What beauty, what scope do they not have! Time, space, infinity, the earth, the sea, the sky, all the elements, the sciences, the arts, all are part of this pleasure. But the mind is too confined by the

3. Hieronymous Fracastorius (1483–1553), Italian physician who expressed in poetry something like the modern view of infectious disease and of fossils. He also described and named syphilis. In his youth, Haller had written a well known, flowery and mildly erotic poem, "Vergnügen an den Wissenschaften," which La Mettrie here parodies.

limits of this world, so imagines a thousand more. The whole of nature is the mind's sustenance: The imagination is its triumph. Let us look at some details.

Sometimes poetry or painting, sometimes music or architecture, singing, dance, etc., ravish connoisseurs with pleasure. Notice Piron's wife Delbar[4] in the loge of the opera. See how in turn her face flushes and pales, how she beats time with Rebel,[5] is moved to pity like Iphigenia, and is enraged like Roland. All the movements of the orchestra ripple across her face like wind on a sail. Her eyes soften, they swoon, laugh, and flash with a warrior's courage. One takes her for a madwoman. She is not, unless it be madness to feel pleasure. She is merely filled by a thousand delights that escape me.

59 Voltaire could not deny tears to his Merope; he knew the value of both his work and the actress.[6] You have read his writings. Unfortunately for him, he cannot read yours. But who does not remember his writings, or have them to hand? And what heart is so hard as to be untouched by them? How could all these delights not make themselves known? Voltaire speaks of them in rapture.

When a great painter speaks of painting, as I have seen with pleasure while reading Richardson's preface these last few days,[7] what eulogies does he not give it? He adores his art, he puts it above everything, he almost doubts that one can be happy if he is not a painter, so enchanted is he by his art!

When reading beautiful passages from the Greek, English, or French tragic poets, or certain philosophic works, who has not been

4. Marie Thérèse Quenaudon (1688–1751), known as Mlle. de Bar, married her long-time companion Alexis Piron (1689–1773), a French epigrammatist and dramatist, in 1741. Oddly, considering what La Mettrie writes, she suffered a nervous attack in 1749 and died insane.

5. François Rebel (1701–1775), who directed the *Opéra* from 1737 to 1747, composed, with his codirector Francoeur, many operas and ballets.

6. Voltaire is the familiar pen name of François Marie Arouet (1694–1778), the French philosopher and writer who was also known in his time as the author of scores of dramas; the tragedy *Mérope* was his greatest moneymaker.

7. Jonathan Richardson (1665–1745), who did portraits of Pope, Newton, Milton, and Steele, and who also published *Essay on the Theory of Painting* in 1715, of which a French translation was published in 1728.

transported as were Scaliger[8] and Father Malebranche.[9] Dacier had never counted on getting what her husband promised her, and yet she got a hundred times more.[10] If one experiences enthusiasm when developing and transmitting the thoughts of others, what can it be to give rise to thoughts oneself? What is this generative force, this giving birth to ideas produced by the taste for nature and the search for truth? How is one to depict this act of will or memory in which, so to speak, the soul reproduces itself by joining one idea to another similar one so a third is born from their resemblance and their union? Just look at the admirable productions of nature. Such is nature's uniformity that nearly all of them are generated in similar ways.

When the pleasures of the senses are badly regulated, they lose all their zing and no longer titillate. The pleasures of the mind resemble sensual pleasures up to a certain point. You must hold them back awhile to sharpen them. Then, study, too, has its ecstasies, just like love. If I may say so, study is a catalepsy or paralysis of the mind, which gets so deliciously inebriated by the object that captivates and enchants it that it seems detached by abstraction from its own body and all that surrounds it, wholly immersed in what it pursues. So much does the mind feel, that it feels nothing. Such is one's pleasure in both seeking and finding the truth. You can judge the power of its charms by the raptures of Archimedes.[11] You know it cost him his life.

Let other men lose themselves in the crowd to avoid knowing, or 60
rather hating, themselves. The wise man flees high society and seeks

8. Joseph Justus Scalinger (1540–1609), classical scholar translator and professor at Leyden, who praised ancient writers with unrestrained enthusiasm.

9. Nicholas de Malebranche (1638–1715), French philosopher and Cartesian who put the claim that animals are machines even more emphatically than Descartes himself. Malebranche was transported by his first reading of Descartes.

10. Anne Tanneguy-Lefèvre Dacier (1654–1720), classical scholar who translated the *Iliad* and *Odyssey,* and who was married to another classical scholar, André, whose production was thought eclipsed by hers.

11. Archimedes (287–212 B.C.). After the Romans breached the defenses of Syracuse, which supposedly had been maintained through a three-year siege by Archimedes' ingenious devices, a Roman soldier came upon Archimedes, who was lost in mathematical contemplation. The soldier ordered him to move on and, when Archimedes failed to respond, killed him.

solitude. Why is he content only with himself or with his peers? Because his soul is an accurate mirror in which his justifiable self-esteem is confirmed in self-contemplation. The virtuous man has nothing to fear from self-knowledge except the dangerous thrill of self-love.

As in the eyes of a man viewing the earth from heaven on high, other men's greatness might disappear, the proudest castles might turn into huts, the largest armies look like a colony of ants fighting with the most ridiculous fury for a grain of wheat—so do all things appear to a wise man, such as you. He laughs at the vain bustling of men whose multitudes crowd the earth and scrabble in pursuit of trifles, from which it rightfully follows that none of them is content.

How sublimely does Pope begin his *Essay on Man*.[12] How petty are men in high places and royalty compared with him! Now you, less my master than my friend, you received from nature the same power of genius as Pope, and you have abused it! You ingrate. You never deserved to excel in the sciences. But you taught me to laugh, like Pope, or rather to groan at the toys and trifles with which monarchs occupy themselves so seriously. I owe all my happiness to you. No, the conquest of the whole world is not worth the pleasure a philosopher enjoys in his study, surrounded by mute friends who nevertheless say to him all he desires to hear. All I ask of God is that he not take from me my health and the necessities of life. Given health, my heart will love life without distaste. Given the necessities of life, my contented mind will always cultivate wisdom.

Yes, study is a pleasure for every age and place, for all seasons,
for every moment. Whom has Cicero not tempted to make of it a
happy trial? Study is a diversion in youth, whose hot passions it
tempers, yet to get full enjoyment from study, I have sometimes
been compelled to abandon myself to love. Love does not frighten
a wise man. Love knows how to show everything to advantage by
uniting one thing with another. The clouds that obscure his under-
61 standing do not make him idle, they only show him the remedy for
getting rid of them. In truth, the sun disperses the clouds in the
atmosphere no more rapidly.

12. Alexander Pope (1688–1744) begins his *Essay on Man*,

> Awake, my St. John! leave all meaner things
> To low ambition, and the pride of Kings.

In old age, that cold season when one is no longer fitted to give or receive other pleasures, what greater resource than reading and meditation! What pleasure to see with one's own eyes the daily formation and growth of work from one's own hands, work that will charm the centuries to come and even one's own contemporaries! "I would like," a man whose vanity was beginning to sense the pleasures of authorship said to me one day, "I would like to spend my life going from my house to the printer's." Was he wrong? And was there ever a doting mother more enchanted to have produced an adorable child than an author who has been acclaimed?

Why heap so much esteem on the pleasures of study? Who does not know that it is a good that does not bring with it the disgust or worries other goods do? That study is an inexhaustible treasure, the surest antidote to bitter boredom, which accompanies and travels with us, that, in short, follows us everywhere? Happy he who has broken the chain of all his prejudices! He alone will taste this pleasure of study in all its purity. Only he will enjoy that sweet tranquility of mind, that perfect contentment of a soul that is sturdy and without ambition. Such is the father of happiness, if not happiness itself.

Let us pause a moment to scatter flowers in the footsteps of these great men, like you, on whom Minerva has placed an immortal crown of ivy. Now Flora invites you to blaze new trails to the icy summit of the Alps to admire with Linnaeus under another snowy peak a garden nature has planted that before was entirely the property of the celebrated Swedish professor.[13] From there you go to those meadows whose flowers await him to arrange themselves in an order they seem until now to have disdained.

There I see Maupertius, the honor of the French nation, whose pleasant company another nation enjoys.[14] He rises from the table of a prince who inspires the admiration or, shall we say, the astonish-

13. Carolus Linnaeus (1707–1778), Swedish botanist whose *Systema naturae* established him as the founder of systematic taxonomy. He classified the chimpanzee in the same genus as the species he dubbed *Homo sapiens*, although he rejected evolution.

14. Pierre Louis Moreau de Maupertuis (1698–1759), French mathematician and champion of Isaac Newton, whom Frederick the Great appointed head of Berlin's Academy of the Sciences in 1746. Some years after La Mettrie wrote these words, Maupertuis clashed with Voltaire, who drove him out of Berlin.

ment of Europe. Where is he going? To the council of nature where Newton awaits him.

What should I say of the chemist, geometer, physician, mechanic,
62 anatomist, etc.? The anatomist gets nearly as much pleasure from examining a dead man as someone once had in giving him life.

But all this is inferior to the great art of healing. The physician is the only philosopher who deserves well of his country. He is like the brothers of Helen in the tempests of life. What magic, what enchantment! The mere sight of him calms the blood, restores peace to the agitated soul, and kindles sweet hope in the mortal hearts of unhappy men. The physician foretells life and death, as an astronomer predicts an eclipse. Each has his own torch to light his way. But if the mind has pleasure finding the rules that guide it, how triumphant you must feel—and you have this happy experience every day—what a triumph when the outcome justifies your boldness!

The first benefit of the sciences comes therefore in their very cultivation. Here already is a real and solid good. Happy is he who has a taste for study! More happy he who, through study, succeeds in delivering his intellect from illusion and his heart from vanity, a desirable goal toward which you were guided by the hands of wisdom at a tender age; whereas so many pedants, after half a century of labor and late nights, bent more by the weight of prejudice than that of time, seem to have learned everything except how to think—a rare skill, to tell the truth, especially among the learned—which ought, however, to be at least the fruit of all the other sciences. Since childhood, I have applied myself solely to this science of thinking. Judge, sir, if I have succeeded. And may you cherish eternally this homage of my friendship for you.

MAN A MACHINE 63

It is not enough for a wise man merely to study nature and the truth. He must also speak out on behalf of the small number of people who want to think and who can think. For it is no more possible for the others, who are willingly slaves of the prejudices, to attain truth, than it is for frogs to fly.

I reduce the systems of philosophy concerning man's soul to two. The first and most ancient is materialism. The second is spiritualism.

Those metaphysicians who suggest that matter might manifest the faculty of thinking have not dishonored reason. Why not? Because they enjoy the advantage (in this case it is one) of expressing themselves poorly. Strictly speaking, to ask if matter sheerly in itself can think is like asking if matter can tell the time. Already we see that we shall avoid this reef, on which Mr. Locke had the misfortune to run aground.[15]

The Leibnizians, with their *monads,* have set up an unintelligible hypothesis. They have spiritualized matter rather than materialized the soul. But how can one define a being whose nature is absolutely unknown to us?

Descartes and all the Cartesians, among whom have long been counted the Malebrancheans, made the same mistake. They said
man consists of two distinct substances, as though they had seen 64
and counted them.

The wisest people say the soul can know itself only by the light of faith. But as rational beings, they believe they have the right to examine what Scripture means by *spirit,* the word used in speaking

15. John Locke (1632–1704) was wrongly (and perhaps willfully) interpreted as a guarded materialist by eighteenth-century French philosophers, Voltaire in particular, in part because Locke wrote that it is as theoretically conceivable that God should add thought to matter as that he should create a separate thinking substance (although elsewhere Locke sees the latter as probable and the former as almost self-contradictory). La Mettrie is here insisting that Locke's supposed materialism leaves thought a mysterious, rather than explicitly mechanical, property of matter.

of the human soul. And if in their inquiries they do not agree with the theologians on this point, are the theologians in any more agreement among themselves on all the others?

Here in a few words is the result of their reflections.

If there is a God, he is the author of nature as of revelation. He has given us the one to explain the other, and reason to reconcile them one with another.

To distrust the knowledge we can draw from animated bodies is to regard nature and revelation as two self-destructive contraries and, consequently, to dare to advance this absurdity: that God contradicts himself in his diverse works and deceives us.

If there is revelation, it cannot therefore contradict nature. Only by nature can we discover the meaning of the words of the Gospel, whose true interpreter is experience alone. Indeed, other commentators up to now have only obscured the truth. We can judge of this by looking at the author of *Spectacle de la nature.*[16] "It is amazing," he says, referring to Mr. Locke, "that a man who so debases our soul as to believe it made of mud, dares appoint reason as judge and sovereign arbitrator of the mysteries of faith." "For," he adds, "what a shocking idea one would have of Christianity if one tried to follow reason."

Besides clarifying nothing concerning faith, these reflections constitute such frivolous objections against the method of those who think they can interpret Sacred Scripture, that I am almost ashamed to waste time refuting them.

65 1. The excellence of reason does not depend on its *immateriality*, a big word empty of meaning, but from its power, extent, and clear-sightedness. Thus, a *soul of mud* that could discern at a glance the relations and consequences of an infinity of ideas that are difficult to understand, would obviously be preferable to a foolish and stupid soul made of the most precious elements. To be a philosopher, it is not enough merely to be ashamed like Pliny of the wretchedness of our origin. Our seemingly base beginning is in fact the most precious thing in the world, for which nature seems to have used the most art and ceremony. But just as man would still be the most perfect of all beings even if he came from a source even more vile in appearance, so is his soul lofty whatever its origin, if it is pure, noble, and

16. Noël Antoine Pluche (1688–1761), a Jansenist abbé and writer. His subsequent works include *Harmonie des Psaumes et de l'Evangile* (1739).

sublime. And this makes whomever is endowed with it worthy of respect.

Mr. Pluche's second way of reasoning seems faulty to me even in his own system, which is a bit tainted by fanaticism. If we have an idea of faith that is contrary to the clearest principles and the most incontestable truths, then we must believe, for the honor of revelation and its author, that this idea of faith is false, and that we do not yet know the meaning of the words of the Gospel.

Of the two possibilities, only one is true: Either all is illusion, nature as well as revelation, or experience alone can make sense of faith. But who is more ridiculous than Pluche? I fancy I hear a Peripatetic saying: "We must not believe Torricelli's experiment, because if we did, if we banish the vacuum, what shocking philosophy will we get?"[17]

I have shown the faultiness of Mr. Pluche's reasoning—it is an obvious *petitio principii*—to prove, first, that if there is Revelation, it is not sufficiently demonstrated by the sole authority of the church *66*
and without any examination by reason, as all those who fear reason claim. To protect from attack the method of those who would like to follow the way I open for them, I propose, second, to interpret supernatural things, incomprehensible in themselves, by the light each of us has received from nature.

We should be guided here by experience and observation alone. They abound in the annals of physicians who were philosophers, but not in those of philosophers who were not physicians. Physician-philosophers probe and illuminate the labyrinth that is man. They alone have revealed man's springs hidden under coverings that obscure so many other marvels. They alone, tranquilly contemplating our soul, have caught it a thousand times in both its misery and its grandeur, without scorning it more in the one state than admiring it in the other. I repeat, these are the only physicians who have the right to speak here. What have others to tell us, above all, theologians? Is it not ridiculous to hear them pronouncing shamelessly on something they are incapable of understanding, from which, on the

17. Evangelista Torricelli (1608–1647), Italian mathematician and physicist who served as Galileo's secretary for the last months of his life. Torricelli invented the thermometer and barometer during the course of his successful attempt to prove that nature's "abhorrence of a vacuum" can be explained mechanically and that a vacuum can be produced artificially.

contrary, they have been completely turned away by obscure studies that have led them to a thousand prejudices, in a word, to fanaticism, which adds further to their ignorance of the mechanism of bodies?

But even had we chosen the best guides, we still would find many thorns and stumbling blocks in our path.

Man is a machine so complicated that it is impossible at first to form a clear idea of it, and, consequently, to describe it. This is why all the investigations the greatest philosophers have made *a priori*, that is, by wanting to take flight with the wings of the mind, have been in vain. Only *a posteriori*, by unravelling the soul as one pulls out the guts of the body, can one, I do not say discover with clarity what the nature of man is, but rather attain the highest degree of probability possible on the subject.

67 Take up, therefore, the staff of experience, and leave behind the history of all the vain opinions of philosophers. To be blind and yet believe that you can do without this staff, is blindness at its darkest. A certain modern thinker was right to say that only conceit keeps one from deriving as much from second as from first causes![18] One can and should admire even the most useless efforts of all those lofty geniuses: the Descarteses, Malebranches, Leibnizes, Wolffs, etc.; but what benefit, I ask you, has anyone gathered from all their profound meditations and works? Let us undertake a search, therefore, not for what has been thought, but for what one must think to attain tranquillity in life.

There are as many different temperaments as minds, characters, and customs. Even Galen knew this, and Descartes went so far as to say that only medical science could change minds and customs as it does the body.[19] It is true that each man is different according to the nature, abundance, and diverse combinations of melancholy, bile, phlegm, blood, etc.

18. The modern philosopher is La Mettrie himself in his *Histoire naturelle de l'âme* (I, 174). For self-protection, he published the book as a purported translation from an English work by a "Mr. Charp."

19. Galen (130?–200?), Greek physician and anatomist whose voluminous works were the ultimate medical authority in Europe until the sixteenth century. He invented the notion that the predominance of certain humors determines personality types. Descartes, in his *Passions of the Soul*, presents a relentlessly mechanical and physiological explanation of the various emotions.

During illness, sometimes the soul disappears and shows no sign of itself; sometimes one would think it had doubled in strength, so much does fury transport it; sometimes imbecility vanishes, and convalescence turns an idiot into a witty man. Sometimes the loftiest genius becomes stupid and no longer knows himself. Goodbye to all that precious knowledge acquired at such great cost and with so much trouble!

Here is a paralytic who asks if his leg is in bed with him; there is a soldier who thinks he still has the arm that was cut off. The memory of his former sensations and of where his soul located them are the sources of his delirious illusion. You need only mention the missing limb to make him recall it and feel all its movements, causing sensations so creepy they can hardly be described in words.

This one cries like a child at the approach of death, while that *68*
one cracks a joke. What would it take to change the intrepidity of Canus Julius, Seneca, and Petronius into pusillanimity or cowardice? An obstruction in the spleen or the liver, a blockage of the portal vein. Why? Because the imagination shuts down with the vital organs, and thence gives rise to the singular phenomena of hysteria and hypochondria.

What could I say that is new about those who imagine they have been transformed into *werewolves, roosters, vampires,* or who believe that the dead suck their blood? Why should I dwell on those who think their noses or other members are made of glass? To restore their use and to show that they are flesh, one counsels their owners to sleep on straw for fear of breakage, and then sets the straw on fire. Sometimes the fear of burning cures paralysis. But I pass quickly over these things known to everyone.

I shall take no longer to detail the effects of sleep. Look at this tired soldier! He snores in the trench to the noise of a hundred cannon! His soul hears nothing, his sleep is perfect apoplexy. A bomb is about to crush him! He will feel this blow less than does an insect underfoot.

On the other hand, that man devoured by jealousy, hate, avarice, or ambition can find no rest. The most tranquil nook, the coolest and most soothing drink, everything is useless to one who has not freed his heart from the torment of the passions.

The soul and the body fall asleep together. As the movement of the blood calms, a sweet feeling of peace and tranquillity spreads through the entire machine; the soul feels itself indolently weighted

down along with the eyelids and collapsing with the fibers of the brain. Thus the soul gradually becomes like a paralytic. The muscles can no longer support the weight of the head; the soul can no longer
69 support the burden of thought; the soul in sleep is as though it does not exist.

The blood circulates too fast? The soul cannot sleep. The soul is agitated? The blood cannot calm down. It gallops through the veins with an audible noise. Such are the two reciprocal causes of insomnia. A single fright in a dream makes the heart beat with redoubled blows and wrenches us out of needed, sweet repose, just like a sharp pain or an urgent call of nature. Finally, just as the mere cessation of the functions of the soul produces sleep, there are frequent half-awake short sleeps of the soul, *daydreams*, even when one is awake, which prove that the soul does not always wait for the body to fall asleep; because if the soul is not sound asleep when daydreaming, it almost is, since it is impossible for it to indicate a single object to which it has paid any particular attention among that countless crowd of confused ideas that like so many clouds fill the atmosphere of our brain.

Opium is too closely related to the sleep it produces not to be included here. This medicine intoxicates, like wine, coffee, etc., each in its own way and according to dosage. Opium transports a man into a state of happiness like that in a tomb, for it is the image of death. What sweet lethargy! The soul would like never to leave it. It was prey to the greatest griefs; now it feels only the pleasure that comes from suffering no more, and enjoys the most charming tranquillity. Opium alters even the will. It forces the soul that wanted to wake up and amuse itself to go to bed in spite of itself. I pass over in silence the history of poisons.

Coffee, that antidote of wine, stimulates the imagination and dissipates our headaches and sorrows, without giving us a hangover the next day as does wine.

Let us contemplate the other needs of the soul.

The human body is a self-winding machine, a living representation
70 of perpetual motion. Food sustains what fever excites. Without food, the soul languishes, goes into a frenzy, and, exhausted, dies. The soul is a candle whose flame is relighted the moment it is put out. But feed the body, pour powerful juices and strong liquors into its pipes, and then the soul arms itself with proud courage, and the soldier, whom water would have made run away, becomes ferocious

and runs gaily to his death to the beat of the drum. It is thus that hot water agitates the same blood that cold water calms.

What power a meal has! It rekindles joy in a sad heart, and joy flows into the souls of guests who sing glad songs in which the French excel. Only the melancholic is overcome, and the scholar is no longer good for anything.

Raw meat makes animals ferocious. Men would be the same if they ate the same meat. This ferocity produces pride in the soul, hate, scorn of other nations, intractability, and other sentiments that deprave the character, just as coarse food makes the mind heavy and dense, lazy and indolent.

Mr. Pope knew well the dominion of gluttony. He says, "The grave Catius always speaks of virtue and believes that whoever tolerates the vicious is vicious himself. These beautiful sentiments last until the dinner hour. Then he prefers a villain who keeps an exquisite table to a frugal saint."

Pope says elsewhere:[20]

> See the same man in vigor, in the gout
> Alone, in company; in place or out;
> Early at business, and at hazard late;
> Mad at a Fox-chase, wise at a Debate;
> Drunk at a Borough, civil at a Ball,
> Friendly at Hackney, faithless at Whitehall.

There was in Switzerland a bailiff named Mr. Steigner de Wittinghofen.[21] He was, on an empty stomach, the most just and even the most indulgent of judges. But unhappy the poor wretch who found himself in the box when Judge Steigner had had a fine dinner! He was then a man who would as soon hang the innocent as the guilty.

Our thoughts, and even whether we are decent men, depend upon

20. Alexander Pope, *Moral Essays*, Epistle I, I, 69. Middlesex members of Parliament were put into nomination at Hackney; once elected they might well betray their constituency at the seat of government in Whitehall.

21. Hans-Ludwig Steiger (1688–1745), proprietor of Wittigkofen, was bailiff of Schenkenberg from 1737 to 1743. La Mettrie makes use of him also in his satire *Le petit homme à longue queue*, in which he imagines Haller introducing his "disciple" La Mettrie to this "excellent before-dinner judge."

71 our gaiety, our bravery; everything depends upon how our machine is wound up. One would say that at certain times the soul dwells in the stomach, and that Van Helmont was not wrong to put its seat in the pylorus,[22] except for taking the part for the whole.

To what excesses cruel hunger can bring us! No respect for the guts to which one owes one's life or to which one has given life! The starving tear them to pieces, make horrible feasts of them, and in the fury that carries them away, the weak is always the prey of the strong.

Pregnancy, that desirable rival of anemia, is not content to drag in its wake the depraved hungers that accompany both conditions. Sometimes it makes the soul carry out the most frightful schemes, the effects of a sudden mania, which suffocates even the natural law. Thus the brain, the mind's womb, is perverted in its own way along with the womb of the body.

And that other frenzy of man or woman hounded by continence combined with good health! It is nothing to this timid and modest girl that she has lost all shame and reserve. Incest is to her no more than adultery to a courtesan. If her needs do not find prompt relief, the effects caused by uterine passion will not stop at mania, etc. No, this unfortunate woman will die of a disease for which there are physicians aplenty.

One need only have eyes to see the necessary influence of age on the reason. The soul follows the progress of the body, as it does education. In the fair sex, the soul also follows refinements of temperament, hence that tenderness, that affection, those keen sentiments, founded more on passion than on reason, those prejudices, those superstitions, whose strong imprint can hardly be erased, etc. Man, on the other hand, whose brain and nerves share the firmness of all solids, has a more sinewy mind, just
72 like his face. Education, which women lack, adds yet new degrees of strength to his soul. With such help from nature and art, how could a man not be more grateful than a woman, more generous, more constant in friendship, more firm in adversity, etc.? But, following pretty much the thought of the author of the *Lettres sur les physionomies*, I note that she who joins the graces of mind and body to the most tender and delicate sentiments of the heart

22. Jan Baptisa Van Helmont (1578–1644) followed Paracelsus in a tradition inherited from antiquity in locating the soul in the stomach.

ought not to envy us men the twin strengths that seem to have been given to man, the one only to better penetrate beauty's charms, the other the better to serve beauty's pleasure.[23]

You don't have to be as great a physiognomist as this author to infer the quality of a mind from strong facial features anymore than you have to be a great physician to recognize a disease by its obvious signs. Examine the portraits of Locke, Steele, Boerhaave, Maupertuis, etc. You will not be surprised to find that they have strong physiognomies and eagle eyes.[24] Look through an infinity of other portraits; you can always distinguish the handsome man from the great genius, and often even the honest man from the knave.

History offers a memorable example of the influence of the weather on man. The famous Duc de Guise was so convinced that Henri II, who had often had him in his power, would never dare assassinate him, that he took off for Blois. Chancellor Chiverni, learning of his departure, cried, "There goes a doomed man." When his fatal prediction was confirmed by the event, everyone asked him how he knew. "I have known the king," he said, "for twenty years. He is good and even weak by nature, but I have observed that a mere nothing irritates him and drives him into a rage when the weather is cold."

The people of this land have a heavy, stupid mind; of that, lively, penetrating, and light. What causes this, if not partly the food they eat, partly their fathers' semen—the history of animals and man shows that the father's semen has sovereignty over the minds and bodies of their children—and partly the chaos of diverse elements *73*
that float in the immensity of the air? The mind, like the body, has its epidemics and scurvy.

Such is climate's dominion that a man who moves to another is affected by the change in spite of himself. He is an ambulatory plant who transplants himself. When the climate changes, naturally the plant sprouts or shrivels.

23. These lines are paraphrased from Jacques Pernetti's *Lettres philosophiques sur les physionomies* (1746), in which he defends a physiological characterization of emotions.

24. Richard Steele (1672–1729) was a British dramatist, journalist, and politician. Hermann Boerhaave (1668–1738) helped make the University of Leyden the preeminent medical center of Europe.

Again, we take on the gestures, accents, and mannerisms, etc. of those with whom we live as automatically as we blink our eyes at the threat of a blow we see coming; or for the same reason a spectator's body automatically imitates, in spite of himself, the movements of a good pantomime.

What I just said proves that the best company for an intelligent man is himself, if he can find no equal. In the company of blockheads, the mind gets rusty for lack of use. In tennis, one's return is rotten when the serve is bad. I would prefer an intelligent man to have had no education at all, provided he is still young enough, than to have been badly educated. A man with a poorly trained mind is like an actor spoiled in the provinces.

The various states of the soul always correlate to those of the body. To better demonstrate this dependence and its cause, I appeal to comparative anatomy. Slit open the guts of man and animals. How can you grasp human nature if you never see how the innards of the one exactly parallel the innards of the other?

The general form and arrangement of the quadruped brain is nearly the same as man's. Same shape, same structure everywhere, with this essential difference: Man has the largest and most convoluted brain of all the animals in proportion to the size of his body. Next comes the ape, then the beaver, elephant, dog, fox, cat, etc. These are the animals that most resemble man, and the corpus callo-
74 sum in each is smaller in the order listed above. Well before the late Mr. de la Peyronie confirmed it with a multitude of experiments,[25] Lancisi said the corpus callosum is the seat of the soul.

After quadrupeds, birds have the largest brains. Fish have large heads, but they are void of sense, like those of many men. Fish have no corpus callosum and very little brain, which is absent in insects.

25. Giovanni Lancisi (1654–1720), an Italian physician who in 1712 based the thesis that the corpus callosum was the "seat of the soul," or of what is common to the senses, on its medial position in the brain and its lack of a bilateral division into a left and right portion. François Gigot de La Peyronie (1678–1747), first surgeon to King Louis XV, argued for the same view on the basis of neurological evidence; autopsies showed that patients who suffered loss of consciousness and sensation had sustained damage to the corpus callosum. La Peyronie published his results in 1741, although he had reported them as early as 1709 in a paper read to the Société des Sciences de Montpellier.

I will not expand in more detail on nature's varieties and theories about them because both are infinite, as one can judge by reading Willis's *De cerebro* and *De anima brutorum.*[26]

I conclude only what follows clearly from these incontestable observations: 1) the fiercer an animal, the smaller its brain; 2) the more docile an animal, the larger its brain seems to become; and 3) a most singular, eternal condition of nature, the more mind gained, the more instinct lost. So which is better, the loss or the gain?

What is more, I do not mean to claim that brain volume alone is sufficient for determining the degree of docility in animals. Quality must correspond to quantity, and the hard and fluid parts must be in that proper balance that constitutes health.

The imbecile does not lack a brain, as is commonly noticed, but it is deficient, for example, by being too soft and of poor consistency. It is the same with madmen; the defects of their brains do not always escape our examination. But when the causes of imbecility, madness, etc., are not visible, where else can we look for the causes of the variety of minds? They would escape the eyes of Argus and the lynx. *A trifle, a tiny fiber, something the most subtle anatomical dissection cannot discover*, would have made idiots of Erasmus and Fontenelle. Fontenelle says so himself in one of his best dialogues.

Besides the softness of the medulla in infants, small dogs, and 75
birds, Willis noticed that the *corps caneles* are effaced, and as though they had faded in all these animals, and that their *striations* are as imperfectly formed as in paralytics. He adds, what is true, that man has a very large annular protuberance; this diminishes by degrees in the ape and the other animals mentioned above, while the calf, ox, wolf, ewe, pig, etc., who have very small annular protuberances, have very large *nates* and *testes.*[27]

26. Thomas Willis (1621–1675), English anatomist and physician who held the Sedlian chair of natural philosophy at Oxford. In the works La Mettrie mentions, Willis frequently compares human and animal brains and roughly succeeds in assigning functions to basic brain divisions such as the cerebrum, cerebellum, and midbrain.

27. Willis believed that the "corps caneles" (*corpora striata*), in connecting the cerebrum, cerebellum, and medulla oblongata, were the seat of the commonality of sense; in paralytics, "softness" is found there. This "annular protuberance" is the pons varolii. The "buttocks" are the superior colliculi, and the "testicles" are the inferior colliculi; we now know that the

No matter how discreet and reserved are the consequences drawn from so many observations of this sort concerning the instability of the vessels and the nerves, etc., so many varieties could not be gratuitous sports of nature. At the very least, they demonstrate the need for an excellent and full organization, since in all the animal kingdom, as the soul grows stronger when the body does, it acquires discernment when the body gains strength.

Let us pause to contemplate the differences in animal docility. Doubtless the most extended analogy leads the mind to believe that all the differences between animals and man are produced by the causes I have mentioned, although I must admit that our feeble understanding, limited to the grossest observations, cannot see the ties between causes and effects. That relation is a sort of *harmony* that philosophers will never understand.

Among the animals, some learn to speak and sing. They remember tunes and hit all the notes as exactly as a musician. Others, who show more intelligence, such as the ape, cannot manage any of this. Surely this is because of a defect in the organs of speech.

But is this defect so basic that one could never correct it? In a word, is it absolutely impossible to teach language to an ape? I do not believe it.

76 I would prefer the orangutan over other apes until by chance we discover some species even more like ours, because there is nothing absurd in such beings existing in regions unknown to us.[28] The

---

superior subserve optical reflexes and the inferior, auditory ones. (La Mettrie's terminology was common in his time: terms for the familiar features of human anatomy were imported to describe the mysterious shapes within the brain.) Willis and La Mettrie took it that the relative size differences reflected the dependence of lower animals (smaller brain) on instinct and higher animals (larger brain) on intelligence and learning.

28. La Mettrie was not in a position to distinguish chimpanzees and orangutans, so "man of the woods" means both, and indeed, in terms of works that La Mettrie might have consulted, the chimpanzee would have loomed larger, even if under the name orangutan. Since he ascribes human intelligence to brain size and finds that the ape most closely approaches human brain proportions; and since he sees language primarily as arbitrary signs for things; he naturally speculates that apes might learn language, thus anticipating the research of the last few decades, which has shown that apes can learn hand signs for things—food items in particular—although they do not develop sentence-making abilities.

orangutan resembles us so closely that naturalists call it *the wild man* or *man of the woods*. I would choose it on the same conditions as those on which Amman chooses students, that is, it should be neither too young nor too old.[29] Those brought to Europe are commonly too old. I would choose the one with the most intelligent physiognomy, and who best performs a thousand little tasks, as promised by that physiognomy. Finally, not being skilled enough myself to be its tutor, I would enroll it in Amman's school, or another as good, if there is one.

From having read his book and those by others who use his method, such as the author of the *Histoire naturelle de l'âme*, you know what marvels Amman has performed on those born deaf. He has, he explains, found ears in their eyes. And in a very short time, he teaches them to hear, speak, read, and write. I grant that the eyes of a deaf person see more clearly and intelligently than if he were not deaf. This is because the loss of one limb or sense augments the strength or penetration of another. But the ape sees and hears, and he understands what he hears and sees. He comprehends so well the signs one makes to him that I have no doubt that at any game or exercise you set the two, the ape will win over students of Amman. Why would the education of apes be impossible? Why could not an ape through careful effort communicate with sign language just like the deaf? I dare not decide whether an ape would be able to talk after we did something to its speech organs, but I would be greatly surprised if it were absolutely impossible. This is because of the great analogy between ape and man, and because no other animal known up to the present time resembles man inside and out *77*
so strikingly. Mr. Locke, who certainly has never been suspected of credulity, had no difficulty believing the story Sir William Temple tells in his memoirs of a parrot who responded appropriately and had learned, like us, to carry on a coherent conversation of sorts.[30]

29. Johann Conrad Amman (1669–1730), Swiss physician who practiced in Amsterdam. He devoted himself to teaching deaf mutes to speak by drawing their attention to the motion of his lips, tongue, and larynx, and getting them to imitate his activity, as he reports in *Surdus loquens* (1692).

30. Locke quotes Sir William Temple's *Memoirs of What Passed in Christendom from 1672 to 1679* in his *Essay concerning Human Understanding* (II, xxvii, 9). Temple speaks to a Prince Maurice who gives an account of a parrot in Brazil who responded appropriately in Portuguese to Maurice's questions in French (according to local interpreters). Writing the *Histoire*

I know that the author of the *Histoire de l'âme* makes fun of this great metaphysician, but if someone had announced to the universe that reproduction can take place without eggs and females, would he have found many partisans? Mr. Trembley, however, discovered such reproduction, which takes place by division alone without coupling.[31] Would not Amman also have been taken to be a madman if, before making his happy experiment, he had bragged that he could teach deaf students successfully, and in such a short time? Nevertheless, his accomplishments astound the whole world, and like the author of the *Histoire des polypes*, he has ascended in full flight to immortality. To my way of thinking, he who performs miracles because of his genius is superior to him who owes his success to chance. He who finds a way of improving the most beautiful of kingdoms by adding new perfections to it deserves elevation above an idle fabricator of frivolous schemes or a toiling author of sterile discoveries. Amman's discoveries are of a higher order of value. He has rescued men from the native condition to which they seemed condemned. He has given them ideas, mind, in a word a soul, which they otherwise would never have had. There is no greater power than that!

Set no bounds on nature's resources; they are infinite, particularly when aided by great art.

Couldn't the same tools that open the eustachian canal in the deaf unplug it in apes? Then might not their welcome desire to imitate their masters free the speech organs in animals who so cleverly and intelligently imitate a multitude of other signs? Not only do I defy anyone to cite any truly conclusive experiment that proves

---

de l'âme under the protective name "Mr. Charp," La Mettrie dismisses Temple's account as fanciful; here he wishes to make the point that startling possibilities should not be dismissed—in particular, the asexual reproduction of the polyp and Amman's success with deaf mutes. Ironically, Professor Irene Pepperburg of the University of Arizona apparently has trained a parrot to speak English in an intelligent manner, with a level of comprehension and usage that seems to exceed what has been achieved in sign language with apes.

31. Abraham Trembley (1700–84), Genevan biologist, whose publication in 1744 on the freshwater polyp showed that it could be sliced into scores of pieces, each of which would carry on as a whole organism, thus suggesting that asexual reproduction is possible and that life (the animating principle or soul) is a property of matter itself.

my project impossible and ridiculous; but the structure and functions 78
of the speech organs in apes are so similar to those in man that I have almost no doubt that if one trained this animal perfectly, one would finally teach it to articulate and, thus, to learn a language. Then he would be no longer either a wild man or a man manqué. He would be a real man, a little man about town, as well set up or muscled as we are for thinking and profiting from his education.

The transition from animals to man is not abrupt. True philosophers acknowledge this. What was man before the invention of words and knowledge of languages? An animal of his species with much less natural instinct than other animals, of which he did not at that time believe himself the king. A man distinguished from the ape and other animals only as the ape himself is distinguished from the other animals, that is, by a physiognomy that shows more discernment than theirs. Reduced to the mere *intuitive knowledge* of the Leibnizians, man saw only figures and colors, without being able to distinguish among them. In old age as in youth, he was always an infant who stammered out his feelings and needs just as a dog who is hungry or bored asks to eat or to be taken for a walk.

Words, languages, laws, sciences, the fine arts arrived, and finally they polished the raw diamond that was our mind. A man was trained like an animal. One became an author the way another became a porter. A geometer learned the most difficult proofs and calculations the way an ape learns to put on and take off his little hat and to mount his trained dog. All was done by means of signs. Each species understood what it was fitted to understand. And thus have men acquired what our German philosophers still call *symbolic knowledge*.

Nothing is so simple, as one can see, as the mechanism of our education! Everything is reduced to sounds or words which fly from the mouth of one through the ear of the other into the brain, which
receives at the same time through the eyes the shapes of the bodies 79
of which these words are the arbitrary signs.

But who was the first to speak? Who the first teacher of humankind? Who invented the technique for capitalizing on our educability? It beats me. The names of those first fortunate geniuses are lost in the dark night of time. But art is the son of nature, which preceded it for a long, long time.

I suppose the best endowed men to whom nature gave all her advantages instructed the rest. They could not have heard a new noise, or experienced new feelings, or have seen the beautiful objects that form the ravishing spectacle of nature, without finding themselves in the situation of Fontenelle's deaf man of Chartres, who heard the astonishing noise of the cathedral bells for the first time when he was forty years old.[32]

Would it be absurd, then, to think that these first mortals tried, like the deaf man or like animals and mutes (another species of animal), to express their new feelings by the management of their imaginations and then by spontaneous sounds proper to each animal, natural expressions of their surprise, joy, transports, or needs? Because, without doubt, those whom nature has endowed with the more exquisite feelings have the greater feeling for expressing them.

I conjecture that that is how men utilized their feeling or instinct to acquire mind, and, in turn, their mind to acquire knowledge. That is the way, as far as I can understand it, man has filled his brain with ideas, for whose reception nature formed it. Nature and man helped each other, and the smallest beginnings grew little by little until we soon perceived everything in the universe as easily as we recognize a circle.

80 Just as a violin string or harpischord key vibrates and produces sounds, so also the strings of the brain echo or repeat the spoken words that produce the sound waves that strike them. But the brain is so constituted that the instant optically well-formed eyes receive the pictures of objects, the brain cannot fail to observe their images and the differences between them. And, when the signs of these details have been engraved on the brain, the soul necessarily sees their relations, which was impossible before the discovery of signs and the invention of languages. In former times, when the universe was virtually mute, the soul saw everything the way a man who has no idea of proportion sees painting or sculpture, without being able to figure them out. The soul was then in its infancy, like a child holding a handful of straw or twigs, seeing them as a bunch but unable to count them or tell them apart. But put a flag or standard numbered "1" on one pole and a flag numbered "2" on another,

32. Bernard Le Bovier De Fontenelle (1657–1757), French writer and secretary of L'Academie des Sciences, who in his *Histoire de l'Académie royale des sciences* (1703, pp. 18-19) gives an account of a man of 23 or 24 years of age, born deaf and dumb, who suddenly heard church bells and rapidly acquired language. He "remembered a purely animal life, completely occupied with present, sensory experience of objects."

and then the child can count them, and soon he will easily learn all of arithmetic. The minute he sees that one number is equal to another according to its *numerical* sign, he will easily conclude that these are two different things, that one and one make two, that two and two make four, and so on. (Even today, there are peoples who, because of lack of a larger number of signs, can count only up to twenty.)

This real or evident similarity of figures is the fundamental basis of all truths and knowledge, among which it is obvious that those whose signs are less simple and less sensible are more difficult to learn than the others. Thus, it takes great genius to embrace and combine the great quantity of words by which the truths about the 81
springs of the sciences of which I speak are expressed, while sciences expressed by figures and other simple signs are easily learned. No doubt, this facility has made the fortune of algebraic calculi, even more than their certitude.

All that learning whose wind inflates the balloon-brains of our proud pedants is nothing more than a vast accumulation of words and figures that impress on our brains all those traces by which we distinguish and recall objects. Ideas rouse one another, as when a gardener looks at a plant he knows well, all its forms flash through his mind. Words and the figures designated by them are so tied together in the brain that one rarely imagines something without thinking of its name or sign.

I always say *imagine* because I believe that everything can be imagined, and that all the parts of the soul can be reduced exactly to imagination alone. Imagination constitutes them all. Thus, judgment, reason, and memory are only parts of the soul that are in no way absolute, but are real modifications of that *medullar canvas* onto which objects painted on the eye are projected as from a magic lantern.

But if such is the marvelous and incomprehensible result of the organization of the brain, if imagination explains everything, and if everything is conceived by it, why do we divide the sensitive principle that thinks in man's mind? Is this not a manifest contradiction for advocates of the simplicity of the mind? If you divide something, it is absurd to continue to claim that it is indivisible. The abuse of language leads to such nonsense, as does the use of those big words *spirituality*, *immateriality*, etc., that even intelligent people scatter about without understanding them.

No system is easier to test than one founded, as mine is, on the

inner feelings and personal experience of each individual. Is the
82 imagination—or that part of the brain that gives rise to fancy whose nature and way of functioning are equally unknown to us—naturally small or weak? It would hardly be strong enough to compare the analogy or similarity among its ideas. It could see only what was right in front of it or affects it most vividly, and then most poorly! But it is still true that only the imagination perceives; the imagination represents all objects with the words and figures that characterize them; and, thus again, the imagination is the soul since it plays all the roles. Thanks to the flattering paint brush of the imagination, the cold skeleton of reason takes on rosy, living flesh. Through the imagination, the sciences flourish and grow in beauty; it makes woods speak, echoes sigh, marble breathe, and rocks cry; all inanimate bodies take on life. It is imagination once again that adds the piquant allure of sensuality to the tenderness of an amorous heart. Imagination causes the germination of sensuality in the dusty studies of philosophers and pedants. Finally, imagination forms learned men as well as orators and poets. Foolishly decried by this one, vainly honored by the other, poorly known by both, the imagination does not merely reign among the graces and fine arts, it does not just paint nature, it measures it as well. The imagination reasons, judges, penetrates, compares, fathoms. Could the imagination feel so deeply the beauties of the paintings traced upon it without noticing the relations among them? No. Just as it cannot enjoy the pleasures of the senses without experiencing their voluptuous perfection, the imagination could not reflect on its mechanically conceived ideas unless it were identical with judgment itself.

Even for the least talented, the more one exercises the imagination or the least genius, the more, so to speak, that genius puts on muscle, the more it grows, becomes alert, robust, vast, and capable of thinking. Even the finest organizations need exercise.

The first virtue of man is his natural constitution. It is in vain
83 that authors of moral treatises do not esteem natural abilities but only talents acquired by reflection and industry. Because where do skill, science, and virtue come from, I ask you, if not from a disposition to skillfulness, learning, and virtue? And again, where does this disposition come from if not from nature? All our estimable qualities come from nature alone; all we are, we owe to nature. Why, therefore, would I not esteem those who have natural virtues, as much as those who shine by acquired, almost artificial virtues? A virtue deserves

esteem whatever it is and wherever it came from. The only question is how to gauge it. The mind, beauty, riches, nobility, although the offspring of chance, all have their value, the same as skill, knowledge, virtue, etc. Those on whom nature has piled her most precious gifts should pity those to whom these gifts have been refused. They can feel their superiority without pride and as connoisseurs. A beautiful woman would be as ridiculous to think herself ugly, as a wise man to think himself a fool. An exaggerated modesty (in truth a rare fault) is a kind of ingratitude to nature. An honest pride, on the other hand, is the mark of a lofty and noble soul, revealed by manly traits that appear to have been formed by feeling.

If constitution is a virtue—the first virtue—and the source of all the others, learning is the second. Without learning, the best constructed brain would be at a complete loss, just as without worldly knowledge, the best-made man would be only a coarse peasant. For what fruit could the most excellent school produce without a womb wide open to the entry and conception of ideas? It is as impossible to plant an idea in a man deprived of sense as it is to make a baby in a woman whom nature distractedly forgot to give a vulva, such as one I have seen who had neither cleft, vagina, nor womb, and who, for this reason, was divorced after ten years of marriage.[33]

But if the brain is well constructed and instructed at the same 84
time, it is like perfectly seeded fertile ground that produces a hundredfold of what is sown. Or (to leave the figurative style that, nevertheless, is often necessary to best express what one feels and to give some grace even to the truth) imagination, elevated by art to the lofty and rare dignity of genius, grasps exactly all the relations of the ideas it has conceived; easily embraces an astonishing host of objects; and finally draws from them a long chain of consequences, which are nothing but further relations begotten by comparison to the first, which the soul finds them to resemble perfectly. That is how, according to my view, the mind is generated. I say the soul *finds* relations, just as I say that the similarity among objects is *obvious;* not that I think for a moment that our senses always deceive us, as Father Malebranche

33. La Mettrie describes this case in his *Système d'Epicure* (XIV). There he uses it to support evolution, arguing that the occasional recurrence of vestigial forms suggests past forms from which the present ones arose through natural selection.

has claimed; or that our eyes are by nature a little drunk and do not see objects as they are in themselves, although microscopes prove this to us every day; but to avoid any dispute with the Pyrrhonians, among whom Bayle has distinguished himself.[34]

I say of the truth in general what Mr. de Fontenelle says of certain truths in particular, that one must sacrifice it to the pleasures of society. The sweetness of my character is such that I avoid all dispute that does not go toward sharpening the conversation. The Cartesians would come to me in vain, charging forward with their *innate ideas*. I would certainly not take a quarter of the trouble that Mr. Locke does to attack such chimeras. Really, why bother to write a big book to prove a doctrine that was set up as an axiom three thousand years ago?

It follows from the principles I have set down and believe to be true, that whoever has the most imagination must be regarded as having the most intellect or genius, because all these terms are synonyms. And, once again, only through shameful inattention to meaning could someone think he is saying different things merely by
85 uttering different words or sounds to which he has attached no real idea or distinct sense.

The loftiest, noblest, and most able imagination is therefore best fitted for the sciences, as well as for the arts. I will not decide whether more intelligence is required to excel in the arts in men like Aristotle and Descartes than in those like Euripides and Sophocles, or whether nature was put to greater expense to make Newton than Corneille (though I strongly doubt it), but it is certain that the imagination alone, diversely applied, produced their distinctive triumphs and immortal glory.

If someone is considered to have little judgment with a lot of imagination, this is because imagination, left too much to itself, almost always looking at itself in the mirror of its sensations, has not adequately acquired the habit of carefully examining these sensations and, so, is more deeply penetrated by their traces or images than by their truth and likeness.

It is true that the springs of the imagination are so lively that if

34. Pyrrhonism derives from the teachings of Pyrrho of Elis (360?–270? B.C.). It is the stance of suspending all judgment, positive or negative, on everything. Pierre Bayle (1647–1706) was a distinguished sceptical writer, who used his scepticism to sever the connection between religion and both reason and morality, moves that La Mettrie approved.

the attention, that key to or mother of the sciences, does not get involved in it, the imagination is barely able to do more than glance at objects and skim over them lightly.

On that branch there, see the bird that seems always ready to fly away? It is the same with the imagination. It is always being carried away by whirlpools of blood and spirits; one wave makes a trace that is wiped out by the one that follows. The soul runs after, often in vain. The soul must expect to lose what it does not quickly seize and nail down. As time's true image, the imagination destroys and renews itself without cease.

Such is the continual, rapid, chaotic succession of our ideas. One drives another away like a wave pushing the wave in front of it, so if the imagination does not sometimes use, so to speak, some of its muscles to maintain its balance on the strings of the brain, to stay with a fleeing object so as not to fall on another until it is time to contemplate it, the imagination will never deserve the lofty name of judgment. In such case, it will express vividly *86*
what it feels vividly. It will form orators, musicians, painters, poets, but not one philosopher. On the other hand, if from childhood one teaches the imagination restraint; keeps it from being carried away by its own impetuosity, which makes only brilliant enthusiasts; trains it to catch and contain its ideas, to turn them in all directions to see all sides of their objects; then the imagination, always quick to judge, through reasoning will comprehend the greatest sphere of objects, and the vivacity of the imagination, always a good sign in children (it is only a matter of regulating it by study and exercise), will develop into that clear-sighted penetration without which one makes little progress in the sciences.

Such are the simple foundations on which the edifice of logic has been erected. Nature laid them down for all humankind, but some people have used them well while others have abused them.

Despite all these prerogatives of man over the animals, man is honored to be ranked among them. To tell the truth, up to a certain age, man is more animal than they, because at birth he has less instinct than they have.

What animal would die of hunger in the middle of a river of milk? Only man. Like that old man, who is still a child of whom a modern thinker speaks after Arnobe, he knows neither what foods are good for him, nor the water that can drown him, nor the fire that can reduce him to ashes.[35] The first time an infant sees a lighted candle, he automatically stretches out a finger to explore this new phenomenon. He learns that it is dangerous at his own cost, but he will not be caught by it again.

Put an infant and an animal on the edge of a precipice. Only the child will fall. He drowns where the animal swims. At fourteen or fifteen, he has hardly a notion of the intense pleasure that awaits him in the course of the reproduction of his species. Already adolescent, he barely knows how to begin the play that nature teaches so
87 quickly to animals. He hides as if he were ashamed to have been created to be happy and feel pleasure, while animals pride themselves on being *Cynics*. Without education, animals are without inhibitions. Look again at this dog and child, who have lost their master on the highway. The child cries, he does not even know which saint to pray to. The dog, better served by his sense of smell than the child by his reason, soon finds his master.

Nature, therefore, made us to be beneath the animals, perhaps better to exhibit the wonders of education, which alone draws us up from the level of animals and finally elevates us above them. But will we say the same about the deaf, those born blind, imbeciles, madmen, wild men, or those raised in the woods by wolves, those whose imagination is corrupted by hypochondria, and finally all those creatures in human shape who have only the coarsest instincts? No. All these men in body, but not in mind, merit no particular classification.

I have no intention of avoiding objections against my opinion that favor a primary distinction between man and the animals. It is said that there is in man a natural law—knowledge of good and evil—which has not been impressed on the hearts of animals.

But is this objection, or rather assertion, based on experience? Philosophers who do not harken to experience can reject anything. So is there some one experience that convinces us that man alone has been illuminated by a light refused to all other animals? If there is none, we can no more know by experience what takes place in

35. The "modern thinker" is La Mettrie in the *Natural History of the Soul.* Arnobius, a third century Christian apologist, had argued that most souls are childish and corrupt, and thus mortal, because he felt that many Christians would not reform themselves unless threatened with total annihilation. With his accustomed jocularity, La Mettrie casts Arnobius as an anticipator of modern materialism.

animals or even in man, than we can fail to feel what affects our inner being. We know we think and experience remorse, because an inner feeling forces us only too much to acknowledge it. But one's own inner feeling is inadequate for judging that someone else experiences remorse. We have to take it on their word that other men feel remorse, or infer it by analogy to the sensible, exterior signs we notice in ourselves when we are plagued by the same tormented *88*
conscience.

To decide whether animals that do not speak have received the natural law, one must, therefore, rely on the signs I have just spoken about, on the assumption that they exist. The facts seem to prove that animals have received the natural law. The dog who bites his master appears to repent the next moment, even though his master had provoked him. He looks sad and upset, does not dare to show himself, and betrays guilt by cringing with a humiliated look. History offers the celebrated example of the lion who refused to tear to pieces a man who had been abandoned to his fury, because he recognized the man as one who had once been his benefactor. Would that man himself always showed such gratitude for good turns, and the same respect for humanity! One would no longer have to fear ingrates or war, the scourge of humankind and the veritable hangman of the natural law.

Consider a being endowed by nature with such precocious and enlightened instinct; a being who judges, plans, reasons, and deliberates as far as the sphere of its activity extends and allows; who is attracted by kindness and put off by abuse that leads him to seek a better master; a being with a structure similar to ours; who does the same things, has the same passions, same sorrows, the same pleasures, more or less acute according to the empire of the imagination and the refinement of the nerves. Would not such a being show clearly that it feels its and our wrongs, that it knows good and evil, and in a word that it is conscious of what it does? Would its soul—which marks like ours the same joys, mortifications, and frustrations—view without repugnance a fellow creature being torn to bits, or piteously shredding him into strips himself? On these grounds, the precious gift of the natural law certainly would not have been refused to animals. They offer obvious signs of their repentance and intelligence. So why would it be absurd to think that such beings, machines nearly as perfect as us, are, like us, made to think and to *89*
feel the natural law working in them?

Let no one object that animals are for the most part ferocious beasts incapable of comprehending the harm they do. After all, do men distinguish any better between virtue and vice? Ferocity is a feature of our species as of theirs. Men who are in the barbarous habit of transgressing the natural law are not so tormented as those who transgress it for the first time and who have not been hardened by the force of habit. It is the same with animals as with man. Both animals and men can be more or less ferocious by temperament, and they become even more ferocious in ferocious company. But a gentle and peaceful animal that lives with animals of its own kind and eats bland food will be the enemy of blood and carnage. If it spills blood, it will blush within. There is this difference, though: Since these gentle and peaceful animals sacrifice everything to the needs, pleasures, and conveniences of life, which they enjoy more than we do, their remorse seems not to need to be so acute as ours, because we are not in the same need as they are. Habit dulls and perhaps stifles remorse, as it does pleasure.

But suppose for a moment I am wrong, that it is not true that nearly everyone else is mistaken on this subject while I alone am right. Then even the most excellent animals do not know the moral distinction between good and evil, they have no memory of the consideration we have for them or of the good turns we have done them, no sense of their own virtues. This lion, for example, of which I have spoken as have so many others, will not remember not wanting to take the life of the man abandoned to his fury for a spectacle more inhuman than anything lions, tigers, and bears would perpetrate among themselves, while our compatriots battle, Swiss against Swiss, brother against brother. They recognize one another, yet en-
90 chain and kill their fellows without remorse, because a prince pays them to murder. So suppose, then, that the natural law has not been given to animals. What follows? Man is not molded out of more precious clay than they. Nature employed the same dough for both man and the animals, varying only the leaven. If, therefore, animals do not repent after violating the inner sentiment of conscience of which I speak, or rather if they are absolutely deprived of it, man must be in the same condition, which means goodbye to the natural law and all the lofty treatises that everyone has published about it! The entire animal kingdom would be deprived of it. But reciprocally, if man cannot refrain from admitting that he always distinguishes, when health lets him be himself, people who are honest, humane,

and virtuous from those who are not; and that it is easy to distinguish virtue and vice from the unique pleasure and peculiar repugnance that seem to be their natural effects; it follows that animals, formed of the same matter, which lacks perhaps only a degree of fermentation to equal man in everything, ought to have the same; and that, therefore, there is no soul or sensitive substance that does not suffer remorse. The following supports these reflections.

The natural law cannot be destroyed. Its imprint is so firm in all animals that I have no doubt whatsoever that the wildest and most ferocious have moments of repentance. I believe that the wild girl of Châlons in Champagne repented her crime, if she truly did eat her sister.[36] The same goes for all who commit crimes involuntarily or compulsively, such as Gaston d'Orleans who could not keep from stealing;[37] or a certain woman who during pregancy was subject to the same vice, which her children inherited; or another pregnant woman who ate her husband; or another who cut her children's throats, salted their flesh, and ate some every day like pickled pork;
or a man-eating thief's daughter, who had lost her father and mother *91*
at the age of one year and was raised by honest folk, and yet took up man-eating herself at the age of twelve; to say nothing of other examples from our observers, which prove that a thousand hereditary vices and virtues pass from parents to children, just as they do in a nurse's milk to suckling babes.[38] I say and I grant that for the most part these unfortunates do not recognize the enormity of their actions while they are doing them. Bulimia, for example, or rabid hunger can overwhelm all sentiment; it is a mania of the stomach that one

36. The *fille sauvage* of Châlons was trapped in a nearby forest in 1731. She was observed catching and eating fish, frogs, and roots, and expressed herself through screeches and howls. She was eventually taught French and she then told of having an older companion with whom she fought shortly before she was captured. La Condamine's *Histoire d'une jeune fille sauvage trouvée dans les bois à l'âge de dix ans* (1755) conjectures that she was an Eskimo who was enslaved and eventually transported to France where she fled her mistress. Many French intellectuals showed an interest in her case.

37. Jean-Baptiste Gaston, duc d'Orleans (1608–1660).

38. Aram Vartanian establishes that La Mettrie derived these various accounts of cannibalism from Hieronymus David Grobius's *Sermo academicus de regimine mentis quod medicorum* (Leyden, 1747), in which Grobius relayed many of the accounts from older texts.

is forced to satisfy. But when they become themselves again, like a sober man after a night of drunkenness, what remorse these women have who recall murdering those they hold most dear! What pangs of conscience for involuntary wrongs they could not resist, that they did not even know they were doing! Apparently, however, this is not enough for the judges. Among the women of whom I speak, one was broken on the wheel and burned, another buried alive. I understand completely what the interest of society demands. But without doubt it would be best if all judges were excellent physicians besides. Only then could they distinguish criminal innocence from criminal guilt. If reason is slave to depraved or maddened senses, how can it govern them?

If the crime brings with it its own proportionately cruel punishment, if the most ingrained and barbarous habitual behavior cannot entirely remove repentance from the hearts of the most inhumane criminals, if they are torn apart by the very memory of their actions, why bother to terrify the imaginations of such weak minds with hell, ghosts, and walls of fire, less real even than the terrors of Pascal? (In a circle or at table, Pascal always needed a rampart of chairs or someone at his left side to keep him from seeing the horrible pits into which he was afraid of falling, whatever understanding he had of these illusions. What a frightful effect of the imagination, or of an idiosyncratic circulation in a lobe of the brain! Genius on one side, half-mad on the other. Madness and wisdom each had its department or its lobe, separated by a longitudinal fissure. On which side was he so attached to the gentlemen of Port-Royal?)[39] Who
92 needs to resort to fables, as a pope himself said in good faith, to torment those unfortunates who are sentenced to die a violent death because a judge does not think them punished enough by their own conscience, which is their chief hangman? It is not that I want to say that all criminals are unjustly punished. I argue only that those whose will is depraved and whose conscience is extinguished are punished enough by their remorse when they come to their senses; by a remorse, again I say it, from which, in such cases, nature really

39. Blaise Pascal (1623–1662), a prodigious mathematician and physicist, became a fearful Jansenist mystic for the last decade of his short life. Pascal's brain showed many lesions and abnormalities after his death. Port Royal, a Jansenist stronghold, was also the center in which Cartesian universal linguistics flourished.

should have delivered unfortunates who were carried away by fatal necessity.

Criminals, the wicked, ingrates, those, in short, who do not feel the pangs of conscience, wretched tyrants unworthy of being born, let them try to wring cruel pleasures from their barbarous behavior. Willy nilly, during calm moments of reflection, their vengeful conscience rises up, testifies against them, and sentences them to nearly ceaseless self-laceration. He who torments other men is tormented by himself, and the ills he causes himself is fair measure of that he causes in others.

On the other hand, there is so much pleasure in causing good and in making others happy, so much contentment from being virtuous, kind, humane, tender, charitable, compassionate, and generous (a word that encompasses all the virtues), that I maintain that whoever is so unfortunate as not to be born virtuous is punished enough.

We were not originally made to be learned. We have become learned, though, by what is perhaps even an abuse of our organic faculties, and that at the expense of the state, which supports a multitude of do-nothings who vaingloriously decorate themselves with the name of *philosopher*. Nature has created us uniquely to be happy, yes, every one of us, from the worm who crawls, to the eagle who loses himself in the clouds. This is why nature has given all animals a share of the natural law more or less refined to fit the needs of the well-tuned organs of each.

Now, how shall we define the natural law? It is a feeling that 93
teaches us what we must not do on the basis of what we would not like someone else to do to us. Dare I add to this common notion that it seems to me that this feeling is only a kind of dread or terror as beneficial to the species as to the individual? Because maybe we respect the purse and the life of others only to assure our own goods, honor, and selves, like those *Ixions* of *Christianity* who love God and embrace so many chimeric virtues only because they fear hell.[40]

You see that the natural law is only an inner feeling of the imagination, as are all other feelings, among which is thought. By consequence, the presence of the natural law obviously presupposes nei-

40. Ixion promised his intended's father rich bridal gifts but burned him to death. Zeus welcomed him to Olympus, where Ixion took the opportunity to ravish Zeus's wife, Hera; Zeus cast him into Hades, bound to a flaming wheel.

ther education, revelation, nor legislator, unless you confound it with civil law in the ridiculous way theologians do.

The weapons of fanaticism can destroy those who witness these truths, but never the truths themselves.

It is not that I call in question the existence of a supreme being. On the contrary, it seems to me that the greatest degree of probability is for it. But because God's existence proves the necessity of one cult no more than that of any other, it is a theoretical truth that is hardly of use in practice. Just as we learn after many experiences that someone's being religious does not mean he is honest, an equal number of experiences authorize us to believe that atheism does not exclude it.

Besides, who knows if the reason for man's existence might not lie in this very existence itself? Perhaps he was cast by chance into a tiny corner of the earth, knowing neither how nor why, but only that he must live and die, like those mushrooms that appear from one day to the next, or those flowers that border ditches and cover walls.

Let us not lose our own selves in contemplating the infinite; we
94 are not made to have the least idea of it. It is absolutely impossible for us to go back to the origin of things. It is all the same for our peace of mind whether matter is eternal or created; whether there is a God or none, we will lose no sleep over it. What madness to torment oneself so much over what is impossible to know, and would not make us happier if we knew it.

But, you say, read the works of people like Fénelon, Nieuwentit, Abadie, Derham, Ray, etc.[41] Well! What can they teach me, or rather,

41. François de Salignac de la Mothe-Fénelon (1651–1715), Archbishop of Cambrai, wrote *Démonstration de l'existence de Dieu, tirée de la connaissance de la nature, et proportionnée à la faible intelligence des plus simples* (*A Demonstration of the Existence of God, Drawn from Knowledge of Nature, and Proportioned to the Most Feeble Intelligence*) (1713). Bernard Nieuwentijd (1654–1718), a Dutch mathematician, wrote a theological treatise that was translated into French under the title *L'Existence de Dieu démontrée par les merveilles de la nature* (*The Existence of God Demonstrated through the Marvels of Nature*) (1725). Jacques Abadie (1654–1725), a French Protestant theologian who lived in exile in England and Ireland for the latter portion of his life, wrote *Traité de la vérité de la religion chrétienne* (*Treatise on the Truth of the Christian Religion*) (1684). William Derham (1657–1735), English divine and naturalist, published *Physico-Theology, or a Demonstration of the*

what have they taught me? These books contain only tedious repetitions by zealous writers, each of whom adds nothing to what the others have said but verbiage, better fitted to fortify than to sap the foundations of atheism. The quantity of proofs drawn from the spectacle of nature does not lend them more force. The structure alone of a finger, an ear, an eye, *one observation of Malpighi* proves it all, and without doubt much better than *Descartes and Malebranche.* Or all the rest proves nothing.[42] The deists and the Christians themselves ought, therefore, to be content to observe that throughout the animal kingdom the same acts of seeing are carried out by an infinity of different means, and all of them perfectly geometrical. With what stronger weapons could one overturn the atheists? If my reason does not deceive me, man and all the animals seem to have been destined to have this unity of views. The sun, the sky, the sea, the natural order, the form of bodies, all are displayed in the eye as in a mirror that faithfully presents the imagination with objects painted upon it following laws that necessitate this infinite variety of images that serve vision. Ears also have a striking diversity in form, without humans, animals, birds, and fish using them differently. All ears are made in such a mathematical way that they all serve the same purpose, that of hearing. Is chance, the deist asks, a great enough geometer to vary at its pleasure the works of which some people think it the author, without so much diversity keeping them from attaining 95
the same ends? Again, the deist raises as an objection those parts in animals that are obviously there for future use: the butterfly in the caterpillar, men in spermatic worms, a polyp that is whole in each of its parts, valves in the heart and lungs in the foetus, teeth in their sockets, and in fluids bones that form and harden incomprehensibly.[43] And these partisans of the deist system, far from neglect-

---

Being and Attributes of God from His Works of Creation (1713). John Ray (1627–1705), an important botanist and taxonomist, also published *The Wisdom of God Manifested in the Works of Creation* (1691).

42. Marcello Malpighi (1628–1694), an Italian physiologist and physician who lectured at the University of Bologna. He was among the first to use the microscope in biology, confirming the existence of the capillaries that Harvey's theory of circulation required. He also found tiny spiral tubes in plant stems.

43. Following his teacher Boerhaave, La Mettrie takes the "spermaticist" view that the human being is preformed in the sperm rather than the ova. Trembly had speculated that large numbers of preexistent polyp seeds were

ing anything useful to it, never tire of piling proof upon proof. They want to profit from everything, sometimes even from weak minds. Look, they say, at people like Spinoza, Vanini, Desbarreaux, Boidin, apostles that are more to the honor of, than to the detriment of, deism![44] The duration of these thinkers' health is the gauge of their atheism. It is in fact rare, the deists say, for unbelievers not to abjure atheism just as soon as the passions weaken along with the body that is their instrument.

Those are certainly the most favorable things one can say concerning the existence of God, although the last argument is frivolous because these conversions are short. The mind almost always returns to its former opinions and conducts itself accordingly just as soon as it has recovered, or rather retrieved, its bodily forces. At least I have just said a lot more about the existence of God than the physician *Diderot* in his *Pensées philosophiques*, a sublime work not likely to convert many atheists.[45] What response can one make to a man who says that we do not know nature at all, that everything could have been produced by hidden causes in her bosom? Look at Trembley's polyp! Does it not contain its own regenerative causes? Would it be absurd, therefore, to think that physical causes explain everything that has happened; that the entire chain of this vast universe is neces-

---

spread through a polyp, thus "explaining" how cutting it into many pieces would produce that many new polyps. The "valve of the oval hole" is an opening in the fetal heart between the right and left auricle that closes after birth.

44. Lucilio Vanini (1585–1619) was burned at the stake in Toulouse for atheism; during his trial he recanted his views although he once more asserted them while burning. Jacques Vallée Des Barreaux (1599–1673), widely regarded as a libertine, experienced several near-death conversions, the first in 1641. Both Baruch Spinoza (1632–1677) and Nicolas Boindin (1676–1751) were regarded as atheists by contemporaries, although there seems to be no creditable evidence of their deathbed conversions. Stories of such conversions abounded in the eighteenth century.

45. Denis Diderot (1713–1784), although not a physician, was the most notable *philosophe* and editor of the *Encyclopédie*. In his *Philosophical Thoughts* (1746), while liberal and anticlerical, he argues that natural science provides the strongest evidence of God's existence. Later, perhaps in part through La Mettrie's influence, Diderot became a straightforward materialist.

sarily tied and subjected to these causes; that nothing that happens could not have happened; and that our absolutely invincible ignorance of these causes drives us to take recourse in a God, who, according to certain people, is not even a *being of reason*? So, to 96
eliminate chance is not to prove the existence of a supreme being, since there could be something else that is neither chance nor God. I mean nature, whose study consequently cannot help but produce unbelievers, as witnessed by the ways of thinking of its most successful investigators.

The *weight of the universe*, far from *crushing* the true atheist, does not even make him stagger. Those signs of a creator we have heard about thousands of times—discerned by a way of thinking elevated above the ordinary—are obvious, however far one pushes the argument, only to anti-Pyrrhonians or to those who have such confidence in their reason as to believe that they can conclude that God exists on the basis of certain appearances; but, as you can see, the atheists can give opposing arguments that are absolutly contrary to theirs, and just as strong. Because if we listen again to the naturalists, they say that the same causes—released by chance mixtures in the hands of a chemist—that produced the first mirror, have in the hands of nature made pure water that serves as a mirror for the simple shepherdess; that the movement that conserves the world created it; that each body has the place nature assigned it; that the same causes spread air around the earth that placed iron and other metals in its bowels; that the sun is a product of nature as natural as electricity, and has no more been made to heat the earth and its inhabitants—which it sometimes burns—than rain was made to sprout grain—which it often spoils; that mirrors and water were no more made so one can look at oneself in them, than any other polished body with the same reflecting properties; that the eye is truly a kind of mirror in which the soul can contemplate images of objects represented in it, but that it is not demonstrated that the eye was made on purpose for such contemplation or placed on purpose in the socket; that, finally, it could well be that Lucretius, the physician Lamy, and all the ancient and modern Epicureans are right when they propose that the eye sees only because it is formed 97
and placed in the socket as it is, and that once the rules of movement followed by nature in the generation and development

of bodies were laid down, it was not possible that this marvelous organ could be organized and placed in any other way.[46]

Such are the arguments for and against the existence of God that will eternally separate the philosophers. I take no sides.

Here is what I said to one of my French friends, as frank a Pyrrhonian as I am, a man of great merit and worthy of a better fate:[47] *Non nostrum inter vos tantas componere lites.*[48] He gave me a most singular response. It is true, he said, that the arguments for and against the existence of God should not disturb the soul of any philosopher who sees that nothing is demonstrated with enough clarity to force his consent, and even the key ideas offered on one side are soon neutralized by the key ideas put forward on the other. However, he continued, the world will never be happy until it is atheist. Here are the reasons this *abominable* man gives. If atheism, he said, were generally widespread, all the branches of religion would be cut off at the root and die. No more wars incited by theological arguments, no more soldiers of religion, terrible soldiers! Then nature infected by a sacred poison would recover its rights and purity. Deaf to all other voices, tranquil mortals would follow only their own spontaneous inner counsel, the only counsel that one cannot scorn with impunity, the only one that can guide us to happiness along the happy paths of virtue.

Such is the natural law. Whoever follows it faithfully is an honest man who merits the confidence of all humankind. Whoever does not follow it scrupulously, no matter how much he affects the trappings of one or another religion, is an impostor and hypocrite, and I would not trust him an inch.

98 But even given all that, there are vain people who think otherwise. They dare affirm that honesty itself demands that they not believe

46. Lucretius (96–55 B.C.) wrote *De rerum natura*, a classical expression of materialism. Bernard Lamy (1640–1685) combined Epicureanism and Cartesianism by stressing that since God's purposes are completely inscrutable to us, we should take up a materialist and determinist view of nature.

47. The "French friend" may well be La Mettrie himself. Two decades later Baron d'Holbach gave systematic expression to this view in his *Système de la nature* (1770).

48. "It is not our part to settle such a great enmity." Vergil, *Bucolics*, III, line 108. La Mettrie may not have settled the matter but he is clearly on the materialist side.

in revelation, but that a religion other than that of nature is still necessary, whatever it may be! How miserable! How pitiful! And what a good opinion they give us of the religion they embrace! We do not solicit here the suffrage of the common herd. Those who set up altars to superstition in their hearts are born to adore idols and not to know virtue.

Now look, all the faculties of the soul depend so much on the proper organization of the brain and of the entire body, since these faculties are obviously just this organized brain itself, there is a well-enlightened machine! Because really, why would man's having a share of the natural law make him any less a machine? A few more cog wheels and springs than in the most perfect animals, the brain proportionately nearer the heart so it receives more blood. The same reasons given, what, finally, am I saying? Unknown causes could produce both this delicate conscience so easy to offend, and this remorse, that are no more foreign to matter than thought is, and, in a word, any other faculty supposed here. Is organization therefore sufficient for everything? Yes, once again. Since thought obviously develops with the organs, why would the matter of which they are made not be susceptible to remorse once it has acquired in time the faculty of feeling?

Soul is, therefore, only an empty word to which no idea corresponds. An intelligent person ought to use it only to name the part in us that thinks. Given the least principle of movement, animated bodies have all they need to move, feel, think, repent, and in a word, to act in the physical world and also in the moral, which depends on the physical.

I assume nothing. For those who think that all difficulties have not yet been removed, here are some experiments and observations that will completely satisfy them.

1. All animal flesh palpitates after death, proportionately longer *99*
   for animals that are colder and perspire less. Turtles, lizards, snakes, etc. are proof of this.
2. Muscles separated from the body, when pricked, retract.
3. Entrails conserve their peristaltic or vermicular movements for a long time.
4. Cowper has shown that a simple injection of warm water reanimates the heart and the muscles.[49]

49. William Cowper (1666–1709) wrote *Myotomia reformata: or, A New Administration of All the Muscles of Human Bodies* (1694).

5. When the heart of a frog is exposed to the sun or, even better, placed on a warm table or plate, it moves for an hour or more after having been removed from the body. Does its movement seem to have stopped irremediably? Just prick it and this hollow muscle will beat again. Harvey made the same observation on toads.[50]
6. Chancellor Bacon, an author of the first rank, speaks in his *Histoire de la vie et de la mort* of a man convicted of treason whose breast was ripped open and his heart torn out alive and thrown into the fire.[51] This muscle first jumped up to a height of a foot and a half, then less high as it lost its strength in each new jump, for seven or eight minutes.
7. Remove the heart from a small chicken still nearly in the egg. The same phenomena as above can be observed in the same circumstances. The heat of one's breath alone is enough to reanimate an animal on the verge of death in a vacuum pump.

   Boyle and Sténon have made these same experiments on pigeons, dogs, and rabbits, of which pieces of the heart move like entire hearts.[52] One sees the same movement in amputated paws of moles.
8. The caterpillar, worm, spider, fly, and eel are the same. The movement of amputated parts is increased in hot water, because of the heat it contains.
9. With one swift sabre cut, a drunken soldier cut off the head
100 of a turkey cock. This animal remained upright, then it walked, and then it ran. Bumping into a wall, it turned about, beat its wings, and continued to run, finally falling down.

50. William Harvey (1578–1657) founded modern physiology by clearly establishing that the heart pumped blood through a circulatory system. Although Harvey made several related experiments animating animal hearts, he made no specific mention of toads.

51. Francis Bacon (1551–1626), British philosopher, administrator, and proselytizer of experimental science, gives this account in his *Historia vitae et mortis* (1623).

52. Robert Boyle (1627–1691), British physicist and chemist, reports such experiments on fish, frogs, and snakes in his *Some Considerations Touching the Usefulness of Experimental Natural Philosophy* (1663). Nicholas Steno (1638–1686), a Danish anatomist and physiologist, reported similar experiments with dogs, rabbits, and pigeons.

All its muscles continued to move while it lay on the ground. I saw it myself, and you can easily see the same thing if you chop off the head of a small cat or dog.

10. Polyps do more than move after being sectioned. In eight days, they reproduce into as many whole animals as there are separate parts. This makes me feel sorry for the naturalist's system of generation, or actually, this discovery pleases me, because it teaches us never to make conclusive generalizations, even from all the best known and most decisive experiments!

So there you have far more facts than anybody needs to prove incontestably that every tiny fiber and piece of an organized body moves according to its own principle, and whose actions, unlike voluntary movements, do not depend on the nerves, since these movements take place without the parts in motion having any communication with the circulation. Now if this force is manifested even in cut up pieces of fiber, the heart, which is composed of specially interlaced fibers, must have the same property. I did not need to read Bacon's *Histoire* to be persuaded of this. It is easy enough to figure out both from the perfect analogy in structure between the hearts of man and animals, and from the compactness of man's heart in which this movement is hidden from the eye only because it is smothered in the heart, and last because in cadavers everything is cold and collapsed. If tortured criminals were dissected while their bodies were still warm, one would see the same movements in their hearts that one observes in the muscles of the faces of people whose heads have been cut off.

This motive principle of whole bodies and of cut up parts is such that it produces movements that are not irregular, as formerly believed, but very regular ones just as much in warm, live, whole animals as in those that are cut up and cold. The only recourse re- 101
maining for our adversaries, then, is to deny thousands of facts that anyone can easily verify.

Where is the seat of this inborn force in our bodies? Clearly it resides in what the ancients call the *parenchyma*, that is to say, in the very substance of the parts, excluding the veins, arteries, and nerves, in short, the organization of the entire body, and that, consequently, each part contains in itself springs whose forces are proportioned to its needs.

Let us consider the details of these springs of the human machine. Their actions cause all natural, automatic, vital, and animal movements. Does not the body leap back mechanically in terror when one comes upon an unexpected precipice? And do the eyelids not close automatically at the threat of a blow? And as I said before, does not the *pupil* contract automatically in full daylight to protect the retina and enlarge to see in the dark? In the winter, do pores of the skin not close automatically so the cold does not penetrate into the veins? Does the stomach not heave automatically when irritated by poison, a dose of opium, and all emetics? Do the heart, arteries, and muscles not contract automatically when one is asleep, just as when one is awake? Do the lungs not automatically work continually like bellows? Do not the sphincters of the bladder, *rectum*, etc. close automatically? Does the heart not contract more strongly than any other muscle, so that the erector muscles raise the rod in man, as they do in animals who beat it on their stomachs, and even in children who have erections if that part is excited? This proves, let me say in passing, that there is in this member an extraordinary spring that is little known and produces effects that have not yet been well explained, despite all the enlightenment of anatomy.

102 I will not comment further on all the small subordinate springs everyone knows about. But there is another, more subtle and marvelous, that animates everything. It is the source of all our feelings, pleasures, passions, and thoughts, for the brain has its muscles for thinking as do the legs for walking. I mean that impetuous autonomous principle that Hippocrates calls ενορμων or the soul. This principle exists and is seated in the brain at the point of origin of the nerves through which it exercises its rule over all the rest of the body. It is the explanatory principle of all that can be explained, including even the surprising effects of the maladies of the imagination.

But to keep from getting bogged down in this ill-understood, teeming swamp, we must limit ourselves to a small number of questions and reflections.

Why does the sight or even the mere thought of a beautiful woman cause such singular movements and desires? Is the behavior of certain organs in this case caused by the nature of these organs? Not at all, but rather by the commerce and sympathy the muscles have with the imagination. There is a first spring excited by what the ancients call the *beneplacitum*, an image of beauty, which excites another spring that is quite dormant until the imagination rouses it. And how is that done, if not by the disordered tumult of the blood and spirits that gallop with extraordinary promptitude to swell the hollow tubes?

Since there are obvious communications between a mother and the child in her womb (at least through the veins, and is it certain there is none through the nerves?); and since it is hard to deny the facts related by Tulpius[53] and other writers who deserve our trust (there is no one who deserves it more); I believe that through such connections the foetus experiences the impetuosity of the maternal imagination, just as soft wax receives all kinds of impressions, and that the traces or cravings of the mother can be imprinted on the
foetus, without being able to understand how it happens, whatever *103*
Blondel and his followers say. Thus, we make amends to Father Malebranche, who was scoffed at far too much for his credulity by authors who have not observed nature closely enough but wanted to subject it to their ideas.

Look at the portrait of the famous Pope, the English Voltaire. The strain, the nerves of his genius are painted on his physiognomy. His face is convoluted, his eyes start out of their sockets, his eyebrows are raised by the muscles of his forehead. Why? Because the origin of the nerves is at work, and because the whole body must be suffering the effects of so difficult a birth. If there were no internal cord pulling the outer ones, from where would these phenomena come? To introduce a *soul* to explain them is to be reduced to depending on the *comings and goings of the Holy Ghost.*

In fact, if what thinks in my brain is not a part of that vital organ, and consequently of the whole body, why does my blood heat up when I am lying tranquilly in bed thinking about my work or reasoning abstractly? Why does the fever of my mind pass into my veins? Ask this of imaginative men, of great poets, of those who are ravished

53. Nicolas Tulp (1593–1674) was Praelector of Anatomy of the Surgeons Guild of Amsterdam and he appears as such in Rembrandt's *Anatomy Lesson*. He reported embryonic malformations in *Observationes medicae* (1652). Malebranche gave theoretical expression to the view that the fetus is influenced by maternal emotions in his *Recherche de la vérité*. James Blondel criticizes this view in his *The Strength of Imagination in Pregnant Woman Examined: and the Opinion That Marks and Deformities in Children Arise from Thence, Demonstrated to Be a Vulgar Error* (1727).

by a well-expressed sentiment, who are transported by an exquisite taste, by the charms of nature, truth, or virtue! It is by their enthusiasm, by the feelings they describe, that you will judge of the cause by the effects. It is by this *harmony* that Borelli, a single anatomist who knew better than all the Leibnizians, confirms the material unity of man.[54] Because, in sum, if the tension of the nerves that causes pain also causes the fever that disturbs the mind and makes it lose its will power; and if, reciprocally, an excessively exercised mind troubles the body and lights that fire of consumption that took Bayle at such an early age; if such and such a titillation forces me to wish for and desire ardently what I cared not a tittle about a moment
104 before; if, in their turn, certain brain traces excite the same itching desire; why consider as two what is obviously only one?[55] In vain does one protest for the sovereignty of the will. For every order it gives, it submits a hundred times to the yoke. And how marvelously the healthy body is forced by a torrent of blood and spirits to obey the ministers of the will, that invisible legion of fluids quicker than lightning and always ready to serve. But just as this power is exercised through the nerves, through them also is it arrested. The strongest will and the most ardent desires of an exhausted lover, will they restore his lost vigor? No, alas! And the will is the first to be punished, since, given certain circumstances, it is not in its power not to want pleasure. What I have said of paralysis, etc., pertains here.

Jaundice surprises you! Do you not know that the color of bodies depends on that of the glasses through which you look at them! Are you unaware that whatever color the humors have, so do the objects, at least in relation to us vain dupes of a thousand illusions. But let the bile flow through its natural strainer to remove this color from the aqueous humor of the eye, and then through the clear eye, the soul will see yellow no more. Similarly, by couching a cataract and

54. Giovanni Alfonso Borelli (1608–1679), an Italian physicist and anatomist, was an early architect of the Cartesian mechanistic approach to animal physiology. Leibniz proposed a "pre-established harmony" between mind and body, supposing that there is no actual causal interaction between the two. La Mettrie means by the "material unity of man" that the mind simply is the brain.

55. Pierre Bayle died in 1706 at the age of 59, probably of tuberculosis. La Mettrie's suggestion that his death had psychosomatic causes seems unwarranted.

injecting the eustachian canal, one returns sight to the blind and hearing to the deaf. During the centuries of ignorance, how many people who were nothing more than clever charlatans passed for great miracle makers? How lofty and powerful the soul and will, which can act only as far as bodily dispositions permit, and whose tastes change with age and fever! Is it any wonder, then, that philosophers have always viewed the health of the body as necessary for the health of the soul? Or that Pythagoras carefully prescribed diet and Plato prohibited wine? Sensible physicians always prescribe a regime that is good for the body as a prelude to improving the mind and elevating it to knowledge of truth and virtue, which are nothing *105*
but meaningless words when one is suffering the disorders of illness and tumult of the senses! Without the precepts of hygiene, Epictetus, Socrates, Plato, etc., preach in vain. All moral philosophy is unavailing for anyone not endowed with sobriety, which is the source of all virtue, as intemperance is of all vices.

Need I say more (and why should I lose myself in the history of the passions when Hippocrates' ενορμων explains them all) to prove that man is but an animal, or a contraption of springs, each of which activates the next without our being able to tell which one nature used to start the merry-go-round of human society? These springs differ among themselves only in location and strength but never in nature. Thus, the soul is only a principle of movement or sensible, material part of the brain, which one can regard as the machine's principal spring without fear of being mistaken. It has an obvious influence on all the others. It even appears to have been made first so that all the others merely emanate from it, as observations on different embryos illustrate.

This natural oscillation specific to every part of our machine and of which each fiber is endowed, and, so to speak, each fibrous element is like that of a pendulum, but it cannot always take place. As oscillation ceases, it must be renewed: It must be strengthened when it weakens and weakened when disrupted by excess of strength and vigor. True health care consists solely in maintaining this balance.

The body is but a clock, and chyle the clock maker. The first move of nature on entering the bloodstream is to excite a fever, which the chemists, always thinking of furnaces, have taken for a fermentation. It increases the filtration of the animal spirits that automatically animate the muscles and heart, as though sent there by order of the will.

106 These animal spirits are the life force that maintains the perpetual movement of solids and fluids for a hundred years, as necessary to the one as to the other. Who can say whether solids contribute more to this performance than fluids, or vice versa? This we know: Each is so necessary to the other that the action of the one would be quickly annihilated without the help of the other. The pressure of the fluids on which their circulation depends activates and maintains the elasticity of the veins. Thus, after death, each substance's natural spring remains more or less strong and survives other manifestations of life to expire the last. So although it is true that the force in the springs of animal parts can be maintained and increased by the circulatory force, it does not depend on the circulatory force since it remains even in amputated limbs and vital organs removed from the body, as we have seen!

I am not unaware that not all experts agree with this, and that Stahl in particular strongly disdains it.[56] This great chemist wants to persuade us that the soul is the sole cause of all our movements. But he talks like a fanatic, not a philosopher.

To refute Stahl's hypothesis, one need not go to the lengths of our predecessors. All you need to do is watch a violinist. What suppleness! What agile fingers! They go so fast that they almost seem not to move at all. Now I ask, or rather defy, those Stahlians who know so much about our soul's abilities, to tell me how the soul could possibly command the execution so quickly of so many movements at a distance in so many different places in the body. If this were possible, it would imply that a flute player could execute brilliant trills on an infinity of stops he does not even know and could not even finger.

But, as Mr. Hecquet says, not everyone is allowed to go to Corinth.
107 Were such prodigies possible, would not Stahl himself have been a better man than chemist and physician?[57] But for that, he (fortunate mortal!) would need a soul different from other men, a sovereign

56. Georg Ernst Stahl (1640–1734), a German chemist and physician, was a vitalist and antimechanist, and the chief opponent of La Mettrie's teacher Boerhaave.

57. Philippe Hecquet (1661–1737) taught medicine at the University of Paris. La Mettrie admired him for his satires on the greed of physicians. The reference is to a line from Horace, "All men may not go to Corinth" (*Epistolae* I, xviv, 36).

soul, which, not content to reign over the *voluntary* muscles, easily takes the reins of the whole body to control, suspend, calm, or excite its movements at will! If such a despotic mistress held in her hands, so to speak, the beating of the heart and the laws of the circulation of the blood, there would without doubt be no fever, pain, or sickliness, no shameful impotence or embarrassing priapism. The soul wills and the springs stand erect or go limp. So how did the springs of Stahl's machine manage to break down so quickly? Whoever is such a great doctor ought to be immortal.

But Stahl is not the only one who rejects the oscillation principle of organized bodies. Greater intellects than he have failed to employ it when they wished to explain the action of the heart, the erection of the *penis*, etc. All one needs to do is read Boerhaave's *Institutions de medicine* to see what excruciating and seductive systems this great man was forced to give birth to out of the sweat of his powerful genius simply because he refused to admit that the heart has such an impressive force.

Willis and Perrault, lesser intellects but assiduous observers of nature (whose work the famous professor from Leiden knew only from others and almost at second hand), seem to have preferred to my principle the assumption of a soul spread generally throughout the body.[58] According to this hypothesis, held also by Virgil and the Epicureans and, at first sight, supported by the case of the polyp, the movements that survive death or dismemberment come from a *vestigial soul* conserved by parts that contract without being stimulated by the blood and animal spirits. From this one can see that these writers, whose solid works easily eclipse all philosophic fables, *108*
were mistaken only the way those are who say matter has the faculty of thinking. I mean they expressed themselves badly in obscure terms that signify nothing. Indeed, what is this *vestigial soul*, if not a poorly labeled Leibnizian motive force, that, nevertheless, Perrault above all really foresaw in his *Traité de la mécanique des animaux*.

Now that it is clearly demonstrated against Cartesians, Stahlians,

58. Both Willis (see notes 26 and 27) and Claude Perrault (1613–1688), a French physician and architect, wrote of a soul spread through the body. La Mettrie notes that the polyp, in being divisible into many self-sufficient parts, tells in favor of such a view. While he condemns such vitalism as obscurantist, he presents it as a step in the right direction, not unrelated to the view he himself espouses in *The Natural History of the Soul*.

Malebrancheans, and theologians (who hardly deserve being placed in such company) that matter is self-moved not only, for example, when organized as in a whole heart, but even when such organization is destroyed, human curiosity would like to know how the original endowment of a body with the breath of life in consequence furnishes it with the faculty of feeling and, finally, with the faculty of thinking? God almighty, what efforts certain philosophers have made to find this out! And what gibberish I have had the patience to read on this subject!

Experience teaches us only that as long as the smallest, moribund power of movement subsists in one or several fibers, only a prick is required to revive and animate it. This is shown by the multitude of experiments I have described to overcome the systems. It is an established fact that movement and feeling excite one another in turn, both in whole bodies and in the same bodies when their structure is destroyed, to say nothing of certain plants that show the same phenomena of union of feeling and movement.

Moreover, how many excellent philosophers have demonstrated that thought is only a faculty of feeling, and that the rational soul is merely the sensible soul applied to the contemplation of ideas and reasoning! This is proved by the sole fact that when feeling is
109 extinguished, so is thought, as in apoplexy, lethargy, catalepsy, etc. It is ridiculous to claim, as some have, that the soul continues to think during soporific illnesses but does not remember its thoughts.

It is foolish to waste time looking for the mechanism of this phenomenon. The nature of motion is as unknown to us as that of matter. There is no way to discover how motion is produced in matter unless, like the author of the *Histoire de l'âme*, one resurrects the ancient and unintelligible doctrine of *substantial forms*![59] I am, therefore, really and truly as content with being ignorant of how inert, simple matter becomes active and compounded into organs, as I am with being unable to look at the sun without red glasses. I am equally tranquil about my ignorance of other incomprehensible marvels of nature, such as the production of feeling and thought in a being that, long ago, seemed to our limited view to be nothing more than a glob of mud.

Grant me only that organized matter is endowed with a motive

59. The author of *The Natural History of the Soul* is La Mettrie himself, writing under the name Charp.

principle, which alone differentiates it from what is not so organized (come on! how could one refuse that most incontestable observation?), and that everything in animals depends on the diversity of this organization, as I have sufficiently proved, and this is enough to solve the riddle of substances and that of man. It is obvious that there is only one substance in the universe and that man is the most perfect animal. Man is to apes and the most intelligent animals what Huygens's planetary pendulum is to a watch of Julien le Roy.[60] If more instruments, wheelwork, and springs are required to show the movements of the planets than to mark and repeat the hours, if Vaucanson needed more art to make his *flute player* than his *duck*, he would need even more to make a *talker*, which can no longer be regarded as impossible, particularly in the hands of a new Prometheus.[61] Similarly, nature had necessarily to employ more art and install more organs to make and maintain a machine that might mark all the throbbings of the heart and mind over an entire century. Because *110*
if the pulse does not show the hours, the body is at least the barometer of heat and vivacity by which one can judge the nature of the soul. I am not mistaken. The human body is an immense clock, constructed with so much artifice and skill that if the wheel that marks the seconds stops because of rust or derailment, the minutes wheel continues turning, as does the quarter hour wheel, and all the rest. Because is not the narrowing of a few veins enough to destroy or suspend the force of movement of the heart, as in the mainspring of a machine, since on the contrary, fluids whose volume is diminished, having less distance to cover, cover it that much faster, as by a new current that the force of the heart augments because of the resistance it

60. Christian Huygens (1629–1695), Dutch physicist, mathematician, and astronomer, designed a mechanical model of the planetary system which, as built by the clockmaker van Ceulen, faithfully indicated the motions of the known planets. Julien Leroy (1686–1759) was a famous French watchmaker who developed a mechanism that automatically adjusted pendulums to temperature changes.

61. Jacques de Vaucanson (1709–1782), a French machine maker, presented his flute player to the French Academy in 1738. He also constructed a mechanical duck and an asp that hissed and darted on a mechanical Cleopatra's breast. La Mettrie was not the only one to suggest that man is a machine that winds its own springs; Descartes was fascinated by mechanical toy men.

finds in the extremities of the veins? When a compressed optic nerve prevents the passage of images of objects, this deprivation of sight no more impedes hearing than, when the functions of the *auditory nerve* are curtailed, deprivation of hearing impedes sight.[62] So is it not because of such blockage that one sometimes hears without being able to say that he hears (unless this is caused by disease), and that someone who can hear nothing but whose lingual nerves are freely active in the brain automatically says out loud everything that passes through his head? These phenomena do not surprise well-informed physicians. They know what to expect of the nature of man. And, to remark in passing, of two physicians, the one who merits the most confidence is, in my opinion, always the one most versed in the physics or mechanics of the human body, the one who occupies himself seriously with pure naturalism alone and ignores the soul and all the anxieties this chimera raises in fools and ignoramuses.

So let the so-called Mr. Charp mock philosophers who regard
111 animals as machines.[63] I beg to differ! I think Descartes would have been a respectable man in all respects despite being born in a century he was not able to enlighten—if he had known the value of experi-

62. The portio mollis is the portion of the eighth cranial nerve that leads into the cochlea of the inner ear, subserving hearing.

63. La Mettrie's *The Natural History of the Soul* (1745) is said, on its title page, to be "translated from the English of M. Charp." When La Mettrie published his *Oeuvres philosophiques* (1751), he included *The Natural History of the Soul* as one of his works but changed its title to *Treatise on the Soul*, perhaps to indicate that it was not based on experimental data. Although La Mettrie excuses Descartes for straying from experiment and observation, Descartes in his *The Passions of the Soul* takes an experimentalist and physiological approach; the letters that accompany the work depict Descartes as hungering for major funding in order to conduct a large scale program of experimental research. Earlier, Descartes had suppressed his *Le Monde*, which contains a hypothetical mechanist account of human bodies. In calling Descartes's dualism a "sleight of hand," La Mettrie further suggests that Descartes was a materialist who believed, as does La Mettrie, that the material body machine is the whole of man. While Descartes most surely believed that the human body is a machine, there is no evidence that he believed that *man* is a machine. Indeed, in the *Passions of the Soul*, he teaches how the mind can control the body. On the other hand, Descartes developed the reflex arc mechanism of stimulus and response that later materialists used to eliminate the mind as unnecessary for explaining body movements.

ment and observation, and the dangers of straying from them. So it is only just of me to make genuine amends to this great man, to make up for all those petty philosophers, pathetic jokers, and Lockean baboons, who, rather than giving Descartes the horselaugh, would do better to acknowledge that without him the field of philosophy, like science without Newton, would still be fallow ground.

It is true that this celebrated philosopher was often wrong, and no one denies it. Nevertheless, he knew animal nature. He was the first to demonstrate fully that animals are pure machines. After such an important discovery, which implies such great intelligence on his part, only a churl would not forgive him his errors!

In my estimation, this great discovery makes up for all his false notes. Because, even though he harps on the distinction between two substances, it is obvious that this is only a shrewd move, a clever stylistic trick to make theologians swallow a poison hidden behind an analogy that everyone sees but them. This impressive analogy forces all scholars and meticulous investigators to admit that however greatly these proud and vain beings desire to exalt themselves, they are at bottom only animals, perpendicularly crawling machines, more distinguished by their pride than by the name of man. These machines have that marvelous instinct that education makes of all the mind, still seated in the brain. If the brain is absent or ossified, then the mind is seated in the medulla oblongata. But the mind is never in the cerebellum, because the mind continues its functions even when the cerebellum is hardened, as others have found, e.g., as Haller shows in the *Transactions*.[64]

To be a machine, to feel, think, know good from evil like blue *112*
from yellow, in a word, to be born with intelligence and a sure instinct for morality, and yet to be only an animal, are things no more contradictory than to be an ape or parrot and know how to find sexual pleasure. And since the occasion presents itself for saying so, who would have ever divined *a priori* that shooting off a gob of sperm during copulation would make one feel such divine pleasure, and that from it would be born a tiny creature who one day, following

64. By La Mettrie's time it was realized that "lower parts" of the brain such as the medulla oblongata could carry on automatic motor functions in absence of the cerebrum and cerebellum. Vartanian reports that the Haller reference is to "Observatio de scirrho cerebelli," *Philosophical Transactions*, 43, no. 474: 100–101.

certain laws, could enjoy the same delights? Thought is so far from being incompatible with organized matter that it seems to me to be just another of its properties, such as electricity, the motive faculty, impenetrability, extension, etc.

You want new observations? Here are some that are incontrovertible, and that prove all of them, that man resembles animals perfectly in his origin, as in every other comparison that I have already believed essential to make.

I appeal to the good faith of our observers. Let them tell us if it is not true that man starts out merely as a tiny worm that turns into a man the way a caterpillar turns into a butterfly. The most serious authors such as Boerhaave in his *Inst.*, *Med.*, etc., tell us what to do to see this animalcule.[65] All inquisitive persons have seen it, like Hartsoeker, in the semen of man, but not in that of woman.[66] Only fools have scruples about the matter. Since each drop of sperm shot into the ovary contains an infinity of these tiny worms, only the most adroit and vigorous has the force to insinuate and plant itself in the woman's egg, which provides its first food. This egg, sometimes caught in the fallopian tubes, is carried through them to the uterus where it takes root like a grain of wheat sown on the ground. But although it becomes immense during the nine months of its growth,
113 it differs in no way from the eggs of other females except that its skin (the *amnios*) never hardens, but is greatly distended, as one can see by comparing a foetus in place and ready to be born (which I have had the pleasure of observing in a woman who died a moment before delivery) with other small embryos very soon after conception. There is always an egg in its shell, and an animal in the egg, confined in its movements, that tries mechanically to see the light of day. To succeed, the little animal begins by breaking this membrane with its head, and it emerges like a baby chick or bird, etc. from the shell. I will add one observation that I find nowhere else. The *amnios* gets greatly stretched but does not get thinner, just like the uterus, which expands with infiltrated juices independently of the bulk and deployment of its vascular convolutions.

65. Boerhaave, *Institutiones rei medicae*, paragraph 651.

66. Nicholas Hartsoeker (1656–1725), Dutch physicist and microscopist, who was one of the first to observe spermatozoa. The advantage the spermaticists had in the debate is that the sperm is animated, while the ova, in not moving, can be regarded as vegetative.

Let us look at man in the shell and out. Examine the youngest embryos of four, six, eight, and fifteen days through a microscope. Older ones you can examine with your naked eyes. What do you see? Just the head, a small round egg with two black points for eyes. Before that, everything being more or less formless, all you can see are the medullary pulp or brain in which the nerve center or principle of feeling forms first, and the heart, which already has the faculty of beating by itself. This is Malpighi's *punctum saliens*, which may already owe some of its vivacity to the influence of the nerves.[67] Then little by little the neck lengthens from the head and dilates to form the *thorax* where the heart has already descended and fixed itself. Then comes the lower abdomen separated by a partition, the diaphragm. One of these dilations produces hands, fingers, nails, and hair; the other produces the lower legs, feet, etc. that support and balance the body, and the only difference one can see in these dilations is their situation. It is an astonishing vegetable growth. Here, hairs sprout from the top of our heads; there, leaves and flowers. The same profusion flourishes everywhere in nature. In the end, *114*
plants have their guiding spirit just as we have our soul, this other quintessence of man.

Such is the uniformity of nature that these observations lead one to recognize the analogies of both the animal and the vegetable kingdoms, and of man to the plants. Are there perhaps even some animal plants like polyps that both vegetate and move about and otherwise function like animals?

This is almost all we know about generation. The various parts that attract one another and were made to join together and reside in such and such a place do join together according to their nature to form eyes, the heart, stomach, and finally, as several excellent men have observed, the whole body. All of this is possible. But because experience forsakes us in the midst of these subtleties, I assume nothing, and regard everything that does not strike my senses as an impenetrable mystery. For example, so rarely do male and female seeds make contact in sexual congress that I am tempted to think that the female seed is unnecessary for generation.

But how can we explain the facts of the matter, that the resem-

67. The *punctum saliens* is the fetal heart, whose appearance in the chick shortly after incubation was described by Malpighi. The term *punctum saliens* was introduced by William Harvey.

blance of children sometimes to the father, sometimes to the mother, without this convenient intercourse between parts? On the other hand, why let lack of an explanation rule out a fact? It seems to me that the male does all the work, both in a woman fast asleep as well as in the most lustful woman. From the beginning, then, the disposition of body parts comes from the male seed or tiny worm. But all this is well beyond the reach of the most excellent observers. Since they cannot see it happen, they can no more imagine the mechanics of body formation and development, than a mole can imagine the path of a running stag.

We are truly moles in the field of nature; we scarcely do more than follow the tracks of this animal. Our pride sets limits where none exist.
115 We are like a watch that a writer of fables might make into a person of consequence in a frivolous book. "What!" this watch would splutter. "That stupid workman made me? Me, who parcels out time! Me, who marks so exactly the course of the sun! Me, who says the hours out loud! Nonsense. That cannot be." Ingrates that we are, we similarly disown the common mother (to use chemical terminology) of all the *kingdoms*. We imagine, or rather suppose, that there is a cause superior to the one we owe everything to, the one that truly has made everything in a manner beyond our understanding. No, nothing is vile in matter except to coarse eyes that fail to comprehend its most brilliant works. Nature is not a shackled worker. She produces millions of men with greater ease and pleasure than a clockmaker has trouble making the most complicated watch. Nature's dazzling power is the same in the production of the vilest insect and the most superb man. The animal kingdom costs it no more than the vegetable kingdom, the loftiest genius no more than a head of wheat. We should judge, then, by what we can see of what is hidden from our eyes and our research, and not make anything up beyond that. Let us follow the performances of the ape, beaver, elephant, etc. If they obviously cannot operate without intelligence, why refuse it to them? And if you grant them a soul whose nature you are unsure about, you fanatics are lost, because then anyone can see that your denial of immortality to animals is gratuitous. Who does not see that a soul must be either mortal, or immortal, like ours, and that all souls must suffer the same fate, whatever it be? And thus the fanatics are *wrecked on Scylla while attempting to avoid Charybdis*.

Break the chain of your prejudices. Arm yourself with the torch of experience. Then you will give nature the honor it merits, rather

than drawing—to nature's disadvantage—no conclusions from the ignorance in which it has left you. If you only open your eyes and put aside what you cannot comprehend, you will see that the plowman whose mind and knowledge extend no farther than the edges of his furrow does not differ essentially from the greatest genius, as *116*
dissections of the brains of Descartes and Newton might have proved. You will be persuaded that the imbecile and nincompoop are beasts in human form, as an ape full of intelligence is just a little man in another form, and finally that because everything depends absolutely on the diversity of organization, a well-put-together animal to whom one has taught astronomy can predict an eclipse just as he can predict the recovery or death of a patient after he has studied in the school of Hippocrates and had experience at the bedside of the sick. On the basis of these observations and truths, we can attribute the admirable property of thinking to matter even without being able to see the connection between the two, because the subject of that thinking is unknown to us.

We cannot say whether all machines and animals perish utterly or take on another form after death, because we know absolutely nothing about it. But to claim that an immortal machine is a chimera or a *being of reason* is to reason as absurdly as would caterpillars, who, on seeing the cast-off skins of their fellows, bitterly deplore the fate of their species that seems to them to be in the process of annihilation. The soul of these insects (because every animal has its own) is too limited to comprehend nature's metamorphoses. Not even the cleverest among them could ever have imagined that he must turn into a butterfly. It is the same with us. Do we know any more of our end than of our beginning? Let us submit ourselves, therefore, to an invincible ignorance on which our happiness depends.

Whoever thinks in this way will be wise, just, and tranquil about his fate, and consequently happy. He will await death neither fearing nor desiring it; he will cherish life barely knowing how disaffection ruins contentment in this happy world; he will be full of respect, gratitude, affection, and tenderness for nature in proportion to the love and benefits he has received from her; and, finally, happy to know nature and to witness the charming spectacle of the universe, he will certainly never suppress nature in himself or in others. Even better! *117*
Full of humanity, he will love nature's traits even in his enemies. Consider how he will treat others. He will pity the vicious without hating them. In his eyes, they will be only counterfeit men. Forgiving the

flaws of their minds and bodies, he will still admire their favors and virtues. Thus, those whom nature has favored will appear to him to merit more consideration than those nature has behaved to like a wicked stepmother. This is why materialists pay homage that everyone else unjustly refuses to natural gifts, which are the source of everything that is acquired. Finally, the convinced materialist, though his own vanity whispers in his ear that he is only a machine or an animal, will not mistreat his fellows. Knowing too well that the inhumanity of their actions is always proportional to their needs, in a word, following the natural law given to all animals, he does not want to do unto others what he would not want them to do unto him.

Let us, therefore, conclude boldly that man is a machine, and that the entire universe contains only one single diversely modified substance. This is not a hypothesis posed to support prior requirements and presuppositions. It is not the work of prejudice or even of my reason alone. I would have disdained a guide that I think so uncertain if my senses, carrying the torch, so to speak, had not obliged me to follow reason by throwing light on it. That is to say, experience has spoken to me on behalf of reason, and so I have joined them together.

But the reader must see that I allow myself only the most rigorous reasoning most directly drawn from a multitude of physical observations that no scientist will call into question. And again I recognize only scientists as judges of the conclusions I draw from this reasoning. I take exception to prejudiced men who are neither anatomists nor knowledgeable about the only philosophy here at stake, that of the human body. Against an oak so solid and firm, what can the feeble
118 reeds of theology, metaphysics, and the schools do? They deploy only toy weapons, like fencing school foils with which one can have fun but never touch an opponent. Need I say that I mean those empty, trivial ideas, those hackneyed and pitiful arguments presented to prove the presumed incompatibility of two substances that in fact touch and move one another all the time, arguments that will be offered as long as there remains even one stain of prejudice or superstition on earth. So there is my system, or rather the truth, short and simple, if I am not very much deceived. Deny it if you can!

Fourth Memoir to Serve as the Natural History of Man

MAN A PLANT 283

Preface

Here is man metamorphosed into a plant. But do not think that this is but a story such as Ovid might have told. On the contrary, the singular analogy between the plant and animal kingdoms has led me to the discovery that the principal parts of men and plants are the same. And if, herein, my imagination plays sometimes, be assured that it is on the table of truth. My field of battle is that of nature, whose legions I reduce to one.

Man A Plant

Chapter One 285

We begin to glimpse the uniformity of nature. Those still feeble rays of light come from the study of natural history. But how far does this uniformity go?

One should never force nature. She is not so uniform that she does not often stray from the laws she favors most. So we will try to see only what there is, without flattering ourselves that we can see everything. Knowing everything is a snare and delusion for vain and unwary minds.

To evaluate the analogy between the two principal kingdoms, one must compare the parts of plants with those of man, and then what goes for man will go for animals, too.

In our species, as in plants, there is a taproot and capillary roots. The lumbar reservoir and the thoracic canal form the one and the lacteous veins the others. They have the same uses and the same functions in both men and plants. Food is carried from the roots throughout the whole organism.

Man is not, as some have said, a topsy-turvy tree with the brain as root, for the brain is just the joining together of the abdominal veins, which are formed first, at least they are before the skin that covers them and forms the bark of man. When one looks at the germ
286 of a plant, one of the first things one sees is its tiny root, and then its stem. One descends, the other rises.

The lungs are our leaves. They do for us what leaves do for plants. Plants have branches to enlarge their lungs so they can get more air, and, because of this, plants, and above all trees, breathe more easily. Why would we need leaves and branches? The number of veins and pulmonary vesicles is so well fitted to the narrow circumference of our body's bulk that there is no need for any more. What a joy it is to observe the blood circulating through these veins, especially in amphibians!

And what resemblance is more striking than those discovered and described by the Harveys of botany? Ruisch,[68] Boerhaave, etc. found in man the same vessels that Malpighi, Loewenhock,[69] and van Royen[70] found in the plants. Does the heart beat in every animal?

68. Frederick Nederlandsch Ruysch (1638–1731), Dutch anatomist and professor at the University of Amsterdam. He was particularly noted for displays produced by injecting colored fluids into blood vessels, bronchial tubes, and capillaries. His *Opera anatomico-medico-chirurgical* was published in 1737.

69. Anton van Leeuwenhoek (1632–1723), Dutch biologist and microscopist, who discovered protozoa, first described spermatazoa, and improved on Malpighi's work. A wizard with his tiny, single lens microscopes, he even observed bacteria in 1683, although it took a hundred years and much better instruments before they could be classified and their significance appreciated.

70. Adrianus van Royen (1704–1779) was a professor of botany at the University of Leyden. He replaced Boerhaave as director of the botanical gardens of Leyden. His *De anatomia et oeconomia plantarum* appeared in 1728.

Does it swell the veins with streams of blood that carry feeling and life throughout the whole machine? Likewise, heat, that other heart of nature, that fire in the bowels of the earth and the sun, a fire that has penetrated the imagination of poets, this fire, I say, is the heart that makes the juices circulate in the tubes of plants, which sweat like men. Indeed, what other cause but heat could make everything in the universe germinate, grow, flourish, and multiply?

Air seems to produce the same effects in plants that are rightly attributed to the subtle spirits in the nerves of man, spirits whose existence is proved by a thousand experiments.

The pressure and spring of air sometimes makes plants elevate themselves above the surface of the water, and open and close as one opens and closes one's hand, a phenomenon that has perhaps given rise to the opinion that ether mixes with the animal spirits *287*
that flow through the nerves.

As flowers have leaves or *petals*, we can view our arms and legs as similar parts. The *nectarium*, which is the reservoir of honey in certain flowers such as the tulip and the rose, is like the breast that contains the milk in the female plant of our species when the male makes it come. The breast in our species is double, and is seated at the lateral base of each *petal* or arm on the large pectoral muscle.

One can regard the womb of a virgin or rather of a woman not yet pregnant or, if you wish, the ovary, as an unfertilized seed. The *stylus* in a woman is the vagina. The vulva or mount of Venus and the odor that exhales from the glands of these parts correspond to the *stigma*. The uterus, vagina, and vulva together form the *pistil*, which is what modern botanists call the female parts of plants.

I make a comparison between the *pericarp* (or seed vessel) and the uterus in a state of pregnancy, because it envelops the foetus. Like the plants, we have our *seed*, and sometimes it is very abundant.

At first glance, the *nectarium* or the breast serves to distinguish the sexes in our species, but the easiest examinations are not always the surest. One must combine the *pistil* with the *nectarium* to obtain the essence of woman, because the *pistil* can well be found without the *nectarium*, but never the *nectarium* without the *pistil*, except in very fat men whose breasts sometimes imitate those of women even to the point of giving milk, as has been observed by Morgagni and many others.[71] Every imperforate woman, if one can call a being

71. Giovanni Battista Morgagni (1682–1771), an anatomist at the University of Padua who has been termed the father of modern pathology.

who has no sex a woman, such as the one I have mentioned more than once, has no breasts. This phenomenon is like the shoot on the vine, especially when it is cultivated.

I leave aside the *calyx*, flower cup, or *corolla*, because man does not have one, as I will explain.

288 Enough of this. I do not want to poach on the preserves of Cornelius Agrippa.[72] I have described botanically the most beautiful plant of our species, I mean woman. If she is wise, although metamorphosed into a flower, she will not be easier to pick.

For us men—and here a glance suffices—sons of Priapus, spermatic animals, our *stamen* is rolled into a cylindrical tube, the *rod*. And the sperm is our fertilizing pollen. Like male plants, we are of the *Monandria*. And women are of the *Monogynia* because they have only one vagina. Finally humankind, in which the male is separated from the female, is of the class *Dieciae*. I use Linnaeus's words derived from the Greek.[73]

I felt obliged to illustrate the analogy between plants and man in their maturity because it is more obvious and easier to understand. But here is a more subtle analogy concerning reproduction in the two kingdoms.

Plants are male and female and in coitus they squirm about like a man and a woman. But what does this important activity that renews all nature consist in? The infinitely tiny globules that issue from the seeds of pollen that cover the stamens of flowers are enclosed like eggs by the shells of these seeds. Needham says this and it is the truth.[74] It seems to me that our drops of semen correspond quite

72. Henry Cornelius Agrippa von Nettesheim (1486–1533), physician and philosopher, who although born in Cologne came to practice medicine in Lyon. He had a popular reputation as a magician.

73. Carolus Linnaeus (1707–1778), Swedish botanist and professor at Uppsala, who established modern systematic taxonomy. He coined the term *Homo sapiens* (Man, wise) and placed the chimpanzee in the same genus (*Homo troglodytes* [Man, cave-dwelling]), although he was quite opposed to evolutionary theory. Subsequent biologists put humans in a biological family separate from the apes, although recent genetic analysis shows that Linnaeus was right.

74. John Turberville Needham (1713–1781), British biologist. In his most famous experiment, Needham carefully sealed boiled mutton broth in glass containers; when he observed thriving microorganisms a few days later, he claimed this was the "spontaneous generation" of life. (Years later, it was

well to plant seeds, and our tiny seminal worms to pollen globules. The animalcules of man are in fact enclosed in two liquids. The juice of the prostate is the more common, and it contains the more precious liquid, the semen proper. And just as in each globule of plant pollen, in each of our seminal worms is contained a miniature human plant. I do not know why Needham took it into his head to deny what is so easy to see. How can a scrupulous physician, a supposed follower of experience alone, dare conclude on the basis 289
of a few observations of a single species that the same phenomena are to be found in another that he has, on his own confession, not observed? Such conclusions were drawn to do honor to a hypothesis, only the name of which is disliked, because he was unhappy that this hypothesis has not yet attained the honor it is due. Such conclusions, I say again, do little honor to their author. A man of Needham's merit has even less need to attack Mr. Géoffroy who, as much as I can judge from his *Mémoire sur la structure et les principaux usages des fleurs*, has more than merely conjectured that plants are fertilized by the pollen from their stamens.[75] I say this in passing.

The juice of plants dissolves better than any other liquid the fertilizing matter so that only its most subtle part hits the target. In the same way, does not the subtlest part of man's semen carry its worms or tiny fish all the way into woman's ovary?

Needham compares the action of the fertilizing globules to that

---

discovered that were the broth boiled for a longer period, generation did not occur; this did not entirely settle the issue, for Needham believed that such a long application of heat would destroy precursors of life.) Though Needham was a Roman Catholic priest, spontaneous generation was widely and naturally regarded as a threat to religion. A French translation of his *New Microscopical Discoveries* (London, 1745) appeared in Leyden in 1747 and has been attributed to La Mettrie.

75. Claude Joseph Geoffrey (1685–1752), French chemist and botanist. Materialist scientists, *philosophes*, and evolutionists of the second half of the eighteenth century often championed spontaneous generation, while religious-minded thinkers and vitalists opposed it. La Mettrie, however, seems undogmatic, for he criticizes some of Needham's effusions and rebuffs his criticism of Geoffrey. (*See* John Turberville Needham, *An Account of Some New Microscopial Discoveries Founded on an Examination of the Clamary and Its Wonderful Milt Vessels; Also, Observations on the Farina Foedeundaus of Plants and an Examination of the Pistil, Uterus, and Stamina of Several Flowers . . .* (London: F. Needham, 1745), pp. 63ff, pp. 72ff.

of a violently heated aeolipile or smoke-driven machine. It also appears like a kind of small eruption, as much in nature as in observation, as in the figure that this young and illustrious English naturalist has drawn of ejaculation in plants.

If it is incomprehensible how the juice peculiar to each plant produces this ejaculation by acting on the seeds of pollen as water does, can we comprehend any better how the imagination of a sleeping man produces emissions by acting on the erector and ejaculator muscles, which even by themselves without help of the imagination sometimes give rise to the same accidents? We can understand this only if the phenomena offered on all sides comes from one cause, I mean a principle of stimulation, which after having stretched the springs, causes them to relax. Without such a principle, pure water and particularly plant juices would no
290 more act on the seeds of pollen than would blood and spirits on the muscles and reservoirs of semen.

The ejaculation of plants lasts only a second or two. But does ours last any longer? I think not, although continence leads to some variations depending on how much sperm is stored in the seminal vesicules. An ejaculation is completed in a single expiration, so it has to be short. Pleasures lasting too long might kill us. Then, because of lack of air or breath, each animal would give life at the expense of its own, and would truly die of pleasure.

In man and plant—same ovaries, same eggs, same fertilizing faculty. Because the smallest drop of semen contains an immense number of tiny worms, it can, as has been observed, carry life to a great number of eggs.

Again, there is the same sterility and the same impotence in men and plants. Just as few truly fertile seeds of pollen hit the target, few animalcules pierce the female egg. But as soon as one is implanted, it is nourished like the globule of pollen; and both form in time a creature of its own species, a man and a plant.

The eggs or seeds of a plant, inappropriately called *germs*, never become foetuses unless fertilized by pollen; similarly, a woman does not produce babies unless a man shoots forth, so to speak, an abridgment of himself into the depths of her womb.

Is it necessary for this pollen to acquire a certain degree of maturity to be fertile? The semen of man is likewise not suited for generation during childhood, perhaps, as the translator of Needham conjectures, because our tiny worms are then in a nymph stage. Infertility results also when one is extremely exhausted, probably because the badly nourished animalcules are too feeble or die. One sows such seeds in vain; plant or animal, they are sterile and produce nothing. Wisdom, then, is the mother of fertility.

The amnios, the chorion, the umbilical cord, the uterus, etc. are *291*
found in both kingdoms. Does not the human foetus by its own efforts come out finally from its maternal prison? So also does the foetus of plants, or to use a neologism, the *embryonic* plant, drop at the least movement as soon as it is ripe. This is the childbirth of plants.

If man is not a plant like *the tree of Diana* and others, he is at least an insect that shoves its roots into the womb just as the fertile seed of a plant shoves its roots into its womb.[76] There is nothing surprising in this idea since Needham observes that polyps, barnacles, and other animals multiply by vegetation. Moreover, do we not prune men like trees? A universally learned author said it before me. That forest of fine men who cover Prussia is due to the late king's study and care. Generosity succeeds still better with the mind. Generosity spurs the mind; it trims it, so to speak, as the trees of Marly, and what is more, as trees that might have been sterile into trees that bear the finest fruit.[77] Is it therefore surprising that today the fine arts take Prussia for their native land? And did not the mind have the right to expect the most flattering advantages from a prince who has so many of them?

Among plants there are also blacks, mulattos, and piebalds, which do not engage the imagination, except perhaps that of Mr. Colonne.[78] Consider the singular plumes, monsters, gnarls, goiters, and the tails of monkeys and birds. Finally, the greatest and most marvelous analogy is that the foetuses of plants nourish themselves,

76. Diana's tree is a branching, tree-like crystallization of silver.

77. The gardens of Marli. Marle (in more recent French, Marne), in English "marl," is a loose, crumbly deposit of limestone and clay sometimes containing fossils of vegetation.

78. Mr. Colonne may be François-Marie-Pompee Colonna (1649–1726), a wealthy and secretive aristocrat whose *Principes de la nature ou de la génération des choses* was published in 1731. Supposedly, he perished when his alchemistical researches set his house on fire.

as Mr. Monro has proved by examining the mechanisms of ovipores and vivipores.[79] Enough said on the analogy of the two kingdoms.

79. Alexander Monro (1697–1767), British anatomist and student of Boerhaave, who with others brought the medical practices of Leyden to Edinburgh, helping to establish it as the Leyden of the English-speaking world, which in turn shaped the medical curriculum of North America. Best known for his anatomical description of the nervous system.

CHAPTER TWO 293

I move on now to the second part of this work—the difference between the two kingdoms.

Plants are rooted in the earth which nourishes them. They have no needs. They fertilize themselves. Lastly, plants are immobile. In sum, plants have been seen as immobile animals that lack intelligence and even feeling.

Although animals are mobile plants, one can consider them as being of an entirely different species because not only do they have the power to move themselves, movement that costs them so little that it even enhances the *health* of the organs on which it depends, but also animals feel, think, and satisfy a multitude of needs with which they are besieged.

The reasons for these variations are found in the differences themselves as indicated by the following laws:

First, the more needs an organism has, the more nature gives it means for satisfying them. These means are diverse degrees of sagacity known as instinct in animals and soul in man.

Second, the fewer needs an organized body has, the less difficult it is to nourish and raise, and the less its share of intelligence.

Finally, it follows from the previous two laws that beings that have no needs have no minds.

An appropriate image of a plant is an infant clinging to its nurse's
nipple, sucking incessantly. Plants are sucklings of the earth, and 294
they leave the breast only when they die. As long as life lasts, plants are tied to the earth; their vital organs mingle with the earth and can be separated from it only by force. They have no problems, no worries about the wherewithal with which to live, and, consequently, they have no such needs.

Plants also make love with no difficulty because, either they carry in themselves a double instrument of reproduction and are the sole hermaphrodites that can impregnate themselves, or, if the sexes are separate in each flower, as long as they are not very far apart, they can get together. Sometimes they engage in coitus at a distance, even when very far apart. The palm tree of Pontanus is not the only example of trees fertilized from a great distance. We have known for a long time that the winds, those messengers of vegetable love, carry the sperm of the males to the female plants. Our sperm runs similar risks, but not ordinarily in the open air.

Not only is the earth the nurse of the plants, but also it is their seamstress. Not content with suckling them, the earth clothes them too. From the same juices with which it nourishes them, the earth spins the clothes that cover them. The *corolla*, of which I have spoken, is adorned with the most beautiful colors. Men and above all women have *corolla* in the form of their clothes and diverse ornaments that cover them during the day, but at night humans are flowers that blossom unbound.

What a difference there is between the plants of our species and those that cover the surface of the earth! Rivals of the stars, plants form the brilliant enamel of the meadows, but they have neither sorrows nor pleasures. How well is everything compensated! Plants die exactly as they live, feeling nothing. It would not have been right for them to live without pleasure, and yet die in pain.

Not only do plants have no soul, but a soul would be useless to them. Having none of the needs of animal life, no worries, no cares,
295 no steps to take, no desires, the least glimmering of intelligence would be as superfluous to plants as light to a blind man. For lack of philosophical proofs, this reasoning, added to sensory experience, counts against the view that plants have souls.

Instinct has been even more legitimately refused to all bodies fixed to rocks and ship bottoms, and to bodies that form in the entrails of the earth.

Perhaps minerals are formed following the laws of attraction such that iron never attracts gold nor gold iron, and that all heterogeneous parts repel each other, and that only homogeneous parts unite to form bodies. But given the darkness that conceals the generation of these things, I come to no conclusions. Just because I do not know how fossils are fabricated, must I invoke or assume a soul to explain how they are formed? It would be pretty strange—especially after denying a soul to organized beings with quite as many blood veins as man—it would be weird, I say, to invest a soul in bodies with simple, plain, and compact structures!

These souls, lavished on all the kingdoms, are nothing but antique, imaginary chimeras. How foolish of modern thinkers to try to fill such souls again with subtle breath! Leave their names and their spirits in peace. To do otherwise would be to abuse the German Galen, Sennert.[80]

All that the modern soul-mongers say is nothing but trifling philosophical games whose only merit is their difficulty, *difficiles nugae*. Must one have recourse to a soul to explain plant growth, which is infinitely faster than that of stones? In the vegetating of all bodies, from the softest to the hardest, does not everything depend on nourishing juices that are more or less earthly and are applied with more or less force to more or less hard masses? On that score, I see, in fact, that a hard rock ought to grow less in a hundred years than a soft plant in eight days.

Besides, we must forgive the ancients for their belief in general and particular souls. Because they did not have experimental physics *296*
and anatomy, they were not versed in the structure and organization of bodies. To them, these bodies were as incomprehensible as a watch is to children or savages who see it for the first time. They do not know its inner workings, so believe it is animated by a soul like their own. But a mere glance at the simple mechanism of this machine is enough to see that its action supposes not the soul of a watch, but rather the soul of an intelligent craftsman, without whom chance would never have marked the hours or the course of the sun.

We are today much more enlightened by physics, which shows us that there is no soul of the world other than God and motion, no soul of plants other than heat. We are more enlightened by anatomy, whose scalpel has worked as well on plants as on us and animals. Finally, more taught by microscopic observations that have laid bare the reproduction of plants, we cannot open our eyes to so many spectacular discoveries without seeing, despite the great analogy shown above, that men and plants differ more than they resemble one another. Indeed, up to the present time, of all known animals, man is the one with the most soul, as he necessarily had to be. And plants, of all beings, unless it be minerals, have and need the least soul. After all, a fine soul, having no concerns about objects, no desires, no passions, no vices or virtues, and above all, no needs, would not even be encumbered with the need to nourish its own body.

80. Daniel Sennert (1572–1637), author of several medical texts that relayed the substantial form tradition, all the sort of thing that La Mettrie now felt should be left to rest in peace and in the past.

After the plants and the minerals, which are bodies without souls, come those beings that begin to be self-animated. Such are the polyp and all animal plants as yet unknown that other fortunate Trembleys will discover in the course of time.

The more bodies have of vegetable nature, the less they have of instinct, and the less their operations suppose discernment.

297 The more they participate in animality, or have functions similar to ours, the more they are generously endowed with this precious gift. In a word, intermediate or mixed beings, as I call them because they are offspring of the two kingdoms, have more intelligence the more they are obliged to move around to find food.

The lowest of animals follows on from the most intelligent of animal plants. I mean the animal that of all the members of this species has the least trouble and expends the least movement in finding its food and its female, but always expends a little more effort than the highest animal plant. This animal has more instinct than the animal plant, even if its extra movement is only a hair's breadth distance. The same goes for all other animals in proportion to the concerns that trouble them. Because without intelligence relative to its needs, to find food this animal could not stretch its neck, that one could not crawl, another could not raise or lower its head, or fly, or swim, or walk. Thus, for lack of ability to make up the losses incurred without cease even by those animals that perspire the least, no animal could continue to live. It would perish as soon as it was born. By consequence, animal bodies would exist in vain, if God had not given to them all, so to speak, that portion of himself that Virgil exalts so magnificently as present in the bees.

CHAPTER THREE 299

Nothing is more charming than the object of our present contemplation, a ladder so imperceptually graduated that nature climbs it without ever missing a step through all its diverse creations. What a tableau the spectacle of the universe offers us! Everything is perfectly placed, nothing is out of order. One goes from white to black through an infinite number of nuances or degrees that render the passage infinitely agreeable.

Man and plants are the white and the black. The quadrupeds, birds, fish, insects, and amphibians are the intermediary shades that soften that striking contrast. Without these shades, without all these graded differences in the animals that I wish to designate under this name, man, this superb animal made of mud like all the others, would have believed himself to be a god upon the earth, and would have adored only himself.

However, there is no animal so paltry and vile whose examination does not diminish the philosopher's pride in himself. If chance has placed us at the top of the ladder, just remember that a trifle more or less in the brain where the soul dwells in all men (except *Leibnizians*) could immediately throw us to the bottom. So do not scorn beings
that have the same origin as man. In truth, they are of second rank, 300
but there they are more secure and stable.

Let us descend, then, from the most intelligent man to the vilest plants, or even fossils. Let us ascend again from the bottom-most of these bodies to the first genius, thereby embracing the entire circle of kingdoms. How admirable everywhere is this uniform variety of nature. Does mind disappear here? There you see it ready to be extinguished like a fire without fuel. Over here, it flares up again and burns brilliantly in us, as the animals' guiding light.

I might introduce here a curious bit of natural history to demonstrate that intelligence has been given to all animals in proportion to their needs. But who needs a plethora of examples and facts? They would only overload us without giving more light, and anyway, the books of those indefatigable observers, the underlaborers of the philosophers, are full of such stuff.

Whoever wants to bore us with all of nature's marvels, go ahead. You, pass your life observing insects. You other, count the small otic bones of the membrane of the gills of fish. If you want, you can even measure how far a flea can jump, not to mention many other miserable creatures. I myself am curious only about philosophy, and only regret being unable to extend its limits. Active nature will always be my only field of observation. I love to see nature at a distance, in the large, in general, but not in particular or in small details. Of course, small details are, to a certain extent, necessary in all the sciences. But devotion to detail is the mark of mediocrity. It is only by observing nature in the large that one can be assured that man is neither entirely a plant nor yet an animal like the others. Must I again reiterate the reason? It is this: Because we have infinitely more needs, it follows necessarily that man must have infinitely more mind.

Who would have believed that such a paltry cause would have
301 produced such grand effects? Who would have believed that our unfortunate subjugation to the importunate necessities of life, which remind us without cease of the misery of our origin and our condition, who would have believed, I say, that they are the source of our happiness, of our dignity, and to go further, even of the sensuousness of the human mind, so superior to that of the human body? Certainly if our needs are, as one cannot doubt, a necessary result of our organic structures, it is no less evident that our soul depends directly on our needs, for it anticipates and satisfies them so alertly that nothing takes priority over them. Even the will must obey them. One can say then that our soul gains force and sagacity in proportion to their multitude, just as a general grows more crafty and valiant the more enemies he has to combat.

The ape obviously resembles man in many other ways than toothwise. Comparative anatomy is proof of this, although teeth were what led Linnaeus to rank man with the quadrupeds, indeed, at their very head. But however easy it is to train this animal, even the most intelligent among them, man still has the greatest learning capacity. We have good reason to speak highly of the accomplishments of animals. Animals certainly deserve to be compared with man. Descartes did them wrong, and he had his reasons. But whatever one says of animals, and whatever prodigies they achieve, they never attain the preeminent status of man's soul. All souls are most certainly baked from the same batter, but ours make by far the better bread. The superior quality and ability of the human soul, its over-abundance of illumination, that obviously result from man's constitution, make man the king of the animals, the only animal suitable for society, the only one to produce language, the only one with the wisdom to establish laws and morality.

It remains for me to forestall a possible objection. First, note that the younger a human baby, the faster it grows and the more needs
it has. So, the objection goes, if the principle that the needs of bodies *302*
are the measure of mind were generally true, why do babies have so little instinct that without a thousand constant attentions they would inevitably perish, whereas animals barely hatched—that hypothetically and in fact have so few needs—are so clever?

This argument is seen to be trifling if one considers that when animals are born, they have already passed a large portion of their short lives in the womb. So when they come out into the world, they are already so well formed that a one-day-old lamb, for example, runs in the meadows and grazes grass like its father and mother.

The man-foetus, on the other hand, spends proportionately much less of its time in the womb, as little as only a possible 1/25 [*sic*, read 1/125] of its long life. So at birth it is not very well formed. It cannot think, and even before it can acquire instincts, its brain must have time to harden, for instincts can no more be settled in an immature brain than sparks can be struck from soft stones. Man, born from parents more naked than any animal, himself more naked and delicate than any animal, cannot reach his peak of intelligence as quickly as animals do theirs. So it fits—intelligence, sorely limited in quickly matured animals, rises to great heights in slowly maturing man. Nothing is lost in waiting. Nature compensates man amply for his slow development by giving him more agile and quick-witted organs.

To form an understanding like ours, nature needed more time than for fabricating animal minds. We had to pass through infancy to reach the age of reason. We had to experience the trials and tribulations of animality to derive from them the advantages that characterize man.

Even if animal instincts were given to a new-born babe, they would never compensate for all the infirmities that besiege its cradle. All the ruses of instinct would fail. Give reciprocally an infant the instinct of the animals who have the most, that baby would not be able even to tie its own umbilical cord, and even less to look for its nurse's

303 nipple. On the other hand, if animals suffered our initial handicaps, they would perish every one.

I have now examined the soul as part of the natural history of animal bodies, but I do not mean to imply that the graduated differences among animals are themselves as novel as the reasons for these gradations. Indeed, how many philosophers, and even theologians, have given animals a soul? So that according to one theologian, the soul of beasts is to the soul of man as the soul of man is to the soul of angels, and always ascending upward, the soul of angels is to the soul of God.